SCRIPTURE:
Quest for Understanding

Daniel Mann
Van Misheff

SCRIPTURE

The Bible versions used in this publication are:

Authors:
Mann, Daniel, and Misheff, Van

SCRIPTURE:
Quest for Understanding

From the book...

> *God has hidden His grace in the midst of the ragged vestures of the broken, in the desperation of the hopeless. Therefore, all who follow Christ—no matter their circumstances—have reason to be of good cheer!*

SCRIPTURE:
Quest for Understanding

Part I

A BACKGROUND
FOR UNDERSTANDING THE BIBLE

continued...

Part II

UNDERSTANDING THE BIBLE

PREFACE

Interpreting and understanding Scripture is a daunting endeavor. What we have tried to do in the writing of this book is help those who read it to roll up their sleeves with fresh confidence and...dig in and study the Bible. There is much work to be done if we are to show ourselves to be approved unto God.

Ah, but if the reader will pray for the Spirit's guidance and blessing and commit to study—helped in some measure by the logic and reasoning of the ideas presented here—there will be a fruitful harvest. For you see, "They [God's ordinances—His Scriptures] are more precious than gold, than much pure gold..." (Psalm 19:10a).

And that is where I come in. Whenever anyone asks me about the writing I do with Daniel, I tell them that my job is simple: I polish the gold! I take the essays from his blogs and do a little "buffing" here, a little "shining" there. I am honored to be on the cover of this book, but the "gold" is all Daniel's. However, I know my friend, and he would be the first to say that any accolades should be directed to God.

The work that we do together is geared towards the goal of enhanced clarity and understanding of Scripture. Our hope is that students of the Word may be edified and strengthened in their faith, with a renewed commitment to share the Good News of our Lord Jesus.

Van

Let us begin our journey together, our
Quest for Understanding...

INTRODUCTION

CHAPTER SUMMARY

Sin is the greatest obstacle to understanding the Word of God. However, God is able to open our minds—supernaturally—so that we are enabled to understand Scripture. In addition, He provides teachers.

There is no need for us to be Bible scholars in order to understand the Word of God. Scripture assures us that Bible comprehension is within the grasp of the ordinary servant of God. Moses told the Israelites that there was no reason for them to claim that they could not understand God's words:

- "For this commandment that I command you today is not too hard for you, neither is it far off. It is not in heaven, that you should say, 'Who will ascend to heaven for us and bring it to us, that we may hear it and do it?' Neither is it beyond the sea, that you should say, 'Who will go over the sea for us and bring it to us, that we may hear it and do it?' But the word is very near you. It is in your mouth and in your heart, so that you can do it." (Deuteronomy 30:11-14)

It was not necessary for the Israelites to perform extreme mental gymnastics so that they could understand the commands of God and, thus, know how they were to live. In fact, as we have just seen, His Word is "very near."

Although there are indeed deep and perplexing challenges of interpretation in the Scriptures, God has promised that, if we ask for wisdom, He will provide it:

- If any of you lacks wisdom, let him ask God, who gives generously to all without reproach, and it will be given him. (James 1:5)

Yet we need to remember that, according to James 1:6-8, if we are double-minded and unredeemed, we will not receive His wisdom. Instead, the Word of God will seem like foolishness to us:

- The natural person does not accept the things of the Spirit of God, for they are folly to him, and he is not able to understand them because they are spiritually discerned. (1 Corinthians 2:14)

We must also keep in mind that sin can blind any of us if we do not repent. The Book of Hebrews is clear in its warning:

- But exhort one another every day, as long as it is called "today," that none of you may be hardened by the deceitfulness of sin. (Hebrews 3:13)

And just how does sin deceive us? If we refuse to repent, we are—in effect—telling God that we know better than He does. When we have this kind of an attitude, we are building a wall against God and the conviction and guidance of His Spirit. Thus, we close ourselves off from any meaningful understanding of Scripture. Spiritually, we calcify and die.

However, our Lord is fully able to open our minds to understanding. This is exactly what Jesus did for His Apostles, who were hiding behind closed doors after He was crucified. Once He had risen from the dead, Christ appeared to them:

- Then he said to them, "These are my words that I spoke to you while I was still with you, that everything written about me in the Law of Moses and the Prophets and the

Psalms must be fulfilled." Then he opened their minds to understand the Scriptures. (Luke 24:44-45)

God can also open our minds. He can help us with the life-long work of interpreting and understanding His Holy Scriptures. After all, according to Ephesians 4:11-14, He has provided His Bride, the Church, with preachers and teachers. It is my hope that this book might serve its readers as one of those "teachers" in our... *Quest for Understanding.*

Daniel

Chapter 1

INTERPRETING SCRIPTURE

CHAPTER SUMMARY
Scripture is both plain and problematic. To adequately understand any one verse, we need to understand every verse.

In some ways, understanding the Bible is as simple as understanding how to read a clock or a calendar. The Bible, including the OT [Old Testament], is often so plain that all Israelite parents—not just those who were priests—were expected to teach its truths to their children:

- These commandments that I give you today are to be upon your hearts. Impress them on your children. Talk about them when you sit at home and when you walk along the road, when you lie down and when you get up. (Deuteronomy 6:6-7)

However, for a number of reasons, interpreting the Bible can also be a challenge:

1. The Bible was originally written in ancient languages. The origins of these languages arose from far different and distant cultures from our own. Even if we rigorously study the Hebrew and the Greek, there are idioms and nuances that we might miss.

2. Our understanding of the Bible may be unduly influenced by our own culture. The influence of culture—its norms, customs and even some of its expectations—can sometimes over-ride our allegiance to Scripture.

3. Some of the Bible is written in figurative, or poetic, language. For example, Jesus spoke in parables:

- Jesus spoke all these things to the crowd in parables; he did not say anything to them without using a parable. So was fulfilled what was spoken through the prophet: "I will open my mouth in parables, I will utter things hidden since the creation of the world." (Matthew 13:34-35, citing Psalm 78:2)

4. To be honest, there are times when we do not want the correct interpretation of the Bible. Often, we prefer an interpretation that will affirm us or our worldview:

- The man without the Spirit does not accept the things that come from the Spirit of God, for they are foolishness to him, and he cannot understand them, because they are spiritually discerned. (1 Corinthians 2:14)

As important as each of these concerns is, in the rest of this chapter, we are going to concentrate on the following challenge to interpreting Scripture:

**The Bible must be understood in its totality
in order for any one part to be adequately understood.**

❖ ❖ ❖

- Jesus answered [Satan], "It is written: 'Man does not live on bread alone, but on *every word that comes from the mouth of God.*" (Matthew 4:4, emphasis added)

As Jesus said, "every word" of Scripture is necessary in order that we might know how to live. In addition, all Scripture is essential for our understanding of the fullness of God's revelation to us. One of Jesus' major critiques of the religious leadership of His day was concerning those who would take one verse out of the context of the rest of the Bible. An unfortunate consequence of this kind of short-sighted handling of Scripture is that the verse would be applied wrongly.

For instance, Israelites were forbidden to work on the Sabbath. And yet as Jesus pointed out, within the Hebrew Scriptures, there were numerous valid exceptions to this rule:

- "Now if a child can be circumcised on the Sabbath so that the law of Moses may not be broken, why are you angry with me for healing the whole man on the Sabbath? Stop judging by mere appearances, and make a right judgment." (John 7:23-24)

The Jewish leadership failed to understand and correctly apply the teachings against work on the Sabbath in light of the exceptions. One of those exceptions was the Mosaic Law's requirement to circumcise male babies on the eighth day. The religious leaders conveniently forgot this exception in their criticism of Jesus.

In order to interpret and apply a verse correctly, it is essential that we have a comprehensive understanding of Scripture. Otherwise, it might seem that Scripture is contradicting itself. Take the example of Jonah preaching to Nineveh:

- On the first day, Jonah started into the city. He proclaimed: "Forty more days and Nineveh will be overturned." (Jonah 3:4)

To our culturally-bound ears, it sounds as if Nineveh was absolutely doomed to destruction in exactly 40 days. However, we later find that this was not the case:

- When God saw what they did and how they turned from their evil ways, he had compassion and did not bring upon them the destruction he had threatened. (Jonah 3:10)

Is this a contradiction? It certainly appears that way; that is, until we read about the gracious conditional quality of many of God's promises:

- "If at any time I announce that a nation or kingdom is to be uprooted, torn down and destroyed, and if that nation I warned repents of its evil, then I will relent and not inflict on it the disaster I had planned." (Jeremiah 18:7-8)

Some might assert that this is simply an example of God—through the words of the prophet Jeremiah—contradicting the Book of Jonah. However, if we understand Scripture in its proper context, we will discover that even Jonah understood the conditionality of God's promise concerning Nineveh. Here is what Jonah said once it became clear to him that Nineveh would be spared:

- "O LORD, is this not what I said when I was still at home? That is why I was so quick to flee to Tarshish. I knew that you are a gracious and compassionate God, slow to anger and abounding in love, a God who relents from sending calamity." (Jonah 4:1-2)

Jonah had so hated Nineveh that he would have been glad to deliver a message promising its unconditional destruction. However, Jonah also knew full well that his God is One who relents.

❖ ❖ ❖

There is another reason why we need to strive to understand the entire counsel of Scripture:

Any statement needs to be understood in context.

I often say, "I love chocolate." While this is true, it does not mean that I *always* love chocolate. In fact, I do not love chocolate after I have already overdosed on sugar. And I most certainly do not love chocolate when I am nauseous.

Do these exceptions mean that my original statement that I love chocolate is wrong? No! It just means that my words must be understood in the context of my life experiences, including even tangential situations with their many nuances. No one would call me a liar for saying that I love chocolate if I declined it when I was not feeling well. Instead, everyone knows that it is perfectly acceptable to state a generalization…*without stating each and every exception along with it*.

Let us consider the example of Jesus' teaching on divorce. In one context, Jesus taught:

- "Anyone who divorces his wife and marries another woman commits adultery, and the man who marries a divorced woman commits adultery." (Luke 16:18)

Does this mean that there were no exceptions to the general rules on divorce and re-marriage? Of course not:

- "But I tell you that anyone who divorces his wife, except for marital unfaithfulness, causes her to become an adulteress, and anyone who marries the divorced woman commits adultery." (Matthew 5:32; see also 19:9).

Whenever a general principle is declared, there is no requirement that all of the exceptions and qualifications must be immediately mentioned along with it.

❖ ❖ ❖

Here is yet another teaching that points out the necessity of understanding the entirety of Scripture. John the Baptist was asked one time if he was Elijah. Basing his answer on the Malachi 4:5-6 prophecy concerning Elijah's return, he denied it. However, Jesus claimed that John was indeed the prophesied Elijah:

- "For all the prophets and the law prophesied until John [the Baptist]. And if ye will receive it, this is Elias [Elijah], which was for to come." (Matthew 11:13-14)

This seems like a clear-cut example of a contradiction. Yet, if we understand this claim within the entirety of Scripture's teaching on the subject, we find that this problem can be resolved. Evidently, Jesus taught that John was Elijah only in a spiritual, or figurative, sense. This becomes apparent in the angel Gabriel's revelation to John's father, Zechariah:

- "...for he [John] will be great in the sight of the Lord. He is never to take wine or other fermented drink, and he will be filled with the Holy Spirit even from birth. Many of the people of Israel will he bring back to the Lord their God. And he will go on before the Lord, *in the spirit and power of Elijah*, to turn the hearts of the fathers to their children and the disobedient to the wisdom of the righteous—to make ready a people prepared for the Lord." (Luke 1:15-17, emphasis added)

It should not be surprising to us that Jesus referred to John the Baptist as Elijah in a figurative, or spiritual, sense. After all, there are a number of instances when Jesus used hyperbole— exaggeration—and other kinds of figurative language. Here are just a few examples:

- "So when you give to the needy, do not announce it with trumpets, as the hypocrites do in the synagogues and on the streets, to be honored by men. I tell you the truth, they have received their reward in full. But when you give to the needy, *do not let your left hand know what your right hand is doing...*" (Matthew 6:2-3, emphasis added)

- "If anyone comes to me *and does not hate his father and mother, his wife and children, his brothers and sisters—yes, even his own life*—he cannot be my disciple." (Luke 14:26, emphasis added)

- "And if your right hand causes you to sin, *cut it off and throw it away*. It is better for you to lose one part of your body than for your whole body to go into hell." (Matthew 5:30, emphasis added)

Thus, we see it once again—diligent study, the correct handling of the Word, and familiarity with the full counsel of the Scriptures can help us on our quest to interpret and understand the Word of God.

❖ ❖ ❖

Finally, let us take a look at Paul's counsel in this matter:

- Do your best to present yourself to God as one approved, a workman who does not need to be ashamed and who correctly handles the word of truth. (2 Timothy 2:15)

Correct Bible interpretation is so foundational to God's purposes that incorrect interpretation is associated with not having God's approval. Let us pray, therefore, that we might handle His Word correctly.

Chapter 2

INTERPRETING SCRIPTURE THROUGH THE LENS OF GOD'S LOVE

CHAPTER SUMMARY

While we are expected to interpret Scripture with the love of God in view, we also need to understand the love of God according to Scripture. If we neglect this crucial step, we might be inclined to interpret "love" in a way that feels right to ourselves. And that interpretation is usually substantially conditioned by our culture.

God is love and, therefore, should we not understand Scripture with His love in mind? Well, yes, of course. But what does God's love entail? A self-identified progressive Christian whom we will call "Bill" insists on reading Scripture in a way that dismisses the verses that Jesus taught on repentance and eternal judgment. As far as Bill is concerned, God's love leaves no room for such "pesky" concepts:

> *I read Scripture through the lens of God's love. I can't believe that a loving God would punish—and certainly, not for eternity.*

In one limited sense, Bill is correct. The way we interpret Scripture should reflect the love of God. The two greatest commandments require us to love God and our neighbor (Matthew 22:37-40). Besides this, the Apostle Paul instructed us to minister Scripture according to God's love:

- As I urged you when I was going to Macedonia, remain at Ephesus so that you may charge certain persons not

17

to teach any different doctrine, nor to devote themselves to myths and endless genealogies, which promote speculations rather than the stewardship from God that is by faith. The aim of our charge is love that issues from a pure heart and a good conscience and a sincere faith. (1 Timothy 1:3-5)

I am sure we would all agree that love must govern our lives, even the way we interpret and teach the Scriptures. However, we must of necessity ask the question, "What does love look like in the Bible?"

Love takes many forms. The prophets of Israel spoke of God's love, frequently manifested in the form of warnings against rebellion. Meanwhile, the false prophets embodied Bill's understanding of love; they invariably preached a popular and comforting message. However, God censured them:

- "They have healed the wound of my people lightly, saying, 'Peace, peace,' when there is no peace. Were they ashamed when they committed abomination? No, they were not at all ashamed; they did not know how to blush. Therefore they shall fall among the fallen; when I punish them, they shall be overthrown," says the LORD. (Jeremiah 8:11-12)

While preaching an indulgent message of peace might have had the appearance and even the "feel" of love, the words of the false prophets failed to penetrate to the core of the problem—the rebellion of Israel. That is why their counterfeit message did not heal; rather, the words of the false prophets allowed the cancer of sin to fester. Therefore, the consequences were bound to be great.

The prophet that truly loved God and His people would preach so that real healing could take place:

- "But if they [the false prophets] had stood in my [God's] council, then they would have proclaimed my words [of warning] to my people, and they would have turned them from their evil way, and from the evil of their deeds." (Jeremiah 23:22)

The false prophets had a perverted understanding of love. They understood only the immediate comfort that their message of "peace" would bring, accompanied by the subsequent approval of men. They had little esteem for the Word of God. Therefore, God chastened them:

- Your prophets have seen for you false and deceptive visions; they have not exposed your iniquity to restore your fortunes, but have seen for you oracles that are false and misleading. (Lamentations 2:14)

A true message of love is one that aims towards people being restored to God through repentance. Inevitably, such a message sounds harsh and unloving. Such was the case when Peter rebuked Simon the Magician, who offered money to purchase the gifts of God:

- But Peter said to him, "May your silver perish with you, because you thought you could obtain the gift of God with money! You have neither part nor lot in this matter, for your heart is not right before God. Repent, therefore, of this wickedness of yours, and pray to the Lord that, if possible, the intent of your heart may be forgiven you. For I see that you are in the gall of bitterness and in the bond of iniquity." (Acts 8:20-23)

After being cut deeply by these words, Simon asked for prayer. Therefore, as we look at the big picture in this story, it turns out that Peter's words—though they might have seemed harsh and unloving—were in fact, loving and merciful.

On another occasion, Peter had preached to a crowd that they were guilty of crucifying Jesus. But this harsh accusation produced fruit:

- "Let all the house of Israel therefore know for certain that God has made him both Lord and Christ, this Jesus whom you crucified." Now when they heard this they were cut to the heart, and said to Peter and the rest of the apostles, "Brothers, what shall we do?" And Peter said to them, "Repent and be baptized every one of you in the name of Jesus Christ for the forgiveness of your sins, and you will receive the gift of the Holy Spirit." (Acts 2:36-38)

Peter did not gloss over the guilt of those with whom he spoke. He went right to the core of their problem and pricked their conscience. This is sometimes what true love looks like.

In the same way, Jesus spoke many harsh words against the religious leadership. For example:

- "But woe to you, scribes and Pharisees, hypocrites! For you shut the kingdom of heaven in people's faces. For you neither enter yourselves nor allow those who would enter to go in. Woe to you, scribes and Pharisees, hypocrites! For you travel across sea and land to make a single proselyte, and when he becomes a proselyte, you make him twice as much a child of hell as yourselves." (Matthew 23:13-15)

Words like these might not seem very loving to us. But if God is love, and everything He does is undergirded with love, then this too is love. When we look at Jesus' words from this perspective, we realize that the leaders whom Jesus was addressing must indeed have needed strong words to penetrate their hardened hearts.

Jesus also spoke harshly to His own disciples:

- But he turned and said to Peter, "Get behind me, Satan! You are a hindrance to me. For you are not setting your mind on the things of God, but on the things of man." (Matthew 16:23)

True love does not always speak soft and comforting messages. True love speaks words that best serve the listener—words like those that God instructed Isaiah to proclaim:

- "Wash yourselves; make yourselves clean; remove the evil of your deeds from before my eyes; cease to do evil, learn to do good; seek justice, correct oppression; bring justice to the fatherless, plead the widow's cause. Come now, let us reason together, says the LORD: though your sins are like scarlet, they shall be as white as snow; though they are red like crimson, they shall become like wool. If you are willing and obedient, you shall eat the good of the land; but if you refuse and rebel, you shall be eaten by the sword; for the mouth of the LORD has spoken." (Isaiah 1:16-20)

Let us return once again to my friend "Bill." His understanding of love is not the Bible's understanding. He is like the false prophets who preached peace when there was no peace. Bill's "love" is not a love that pleases God. It is a love that cannot heal because it declares words that do not come from God, or His Word. We need to reject this kind of easy love and learn to appreciate the tough love of God.

God exercised this kind of love in regard to the sin of Ananias and Sapphira. They were the couple who had given half of the proceeds of the sale of their property to the Apostles. The problem that arose was that they had lied to the Holy Spirit in the process. They claimed that they had given all that they had earned from the sale when they had in fact only given half. Because of this, God struck them dead, and the people were terrified by His show of judgment. However, instead of a crippling blow, God's punitive action seems to have revived the early church:

- And great fear came upon the whole church and upon all who heard of these things. Now many signs and wonders were regularly done among the people by the hands of the apostles. And they were all together in Solomon's Portico. None of the rest dared join them, but the people held them in high esteem. And more than ever believers were added to the Lord, multitudes of both men and women... (Acts 5:11-14)

It is plain to see that the love of God should not cause us to gloss over His judgments. Rather, we should acknowledge and affirm them, even as we affirm the rest of Scripture.

❖ ❖ ❖

It would be good for us to remember always that faithfulness to Scripture is faithfulness to God. We should never try to impose our own philosophy upon Scripture. We should always try to understand God's Word as He intended it to be understood. In fact, we are commanded to rightly interpret God's precious Word:

- Do your best to present yourself to God as one approved, a worker who has no need to be ashamed, rightly handling the word of truth. (2 Timothy 2:15)

Although the message of this verse is crystal-clear, we can easily find ourselves slipping into less valid ways of living out our theology. For the first several years of my Christian walk, I interpreted Scripture through a distorted lens. I tried to understand the Word in a way that would enable me to feel good about myself, not thinking for a moment that there was anything wrong with this manner of interpretation.

If my perspective on a verse felt right to me, I would embrace it. If it didn't, I would try to interpret it in a more comfortable way. If that didn't work, I would simply ignore it.

This errant way of reading Scripture was no different from the way I had read it before I was saved. Ethnically a Jew and a Zionist living in Israel, my favorite book quickly became the Book of Joshua. Why? Because my people were victorious over all their enemies, and that made me feel good!

However, the next book was Judges. Expecting more of the same ego-enhancement I had received from Joshua, I quickly became very disappointed with what I was reading. My solution? I gave up reading any of the Hebrew Scriptures.

I believe that many Christians are doing the same thing. We comb the Word, looking for support for our own conclusions. Even Bible scholars can fall into this trap. One theologian made the claim that Jesus had admitted that He was wrong about the Canaanite woman in Matthew 15. According to the theologian, at first Jesus had thought that the woman was not worthy of receiving anything from Him. However, after seeing her faith, He decided otherwise.

Because of his misguided understanding of this incident, the theologian declared that Scripture is often wrong. He claimed that the perception of truth in that situation had evolved as Jesus' understanding had evolved. Furthermore, if Jesus' understanding had evolved, then Scripture was also in the process of evolving. Consequently, much of what is written in Scripture is faulty. Therefore, this theologian concluded that, ultimately, *we* must decide what we are to believe. According to this line of thinking, *we* become the judges of Scripture, instead of Scripture judging us. Our judgment thus reigns supreme.

And, if our judgment is supreme, then why should we even bother with the Scriptures?

❖ ❖ ❖

In some ways, Scripture has become the servant of our lifestyles. We coerce the Word to say the very things that will justify the way we have chosen to live. For example, Christians who believe in socialism or communism are quick to exalt the few verses that show that the early church disciples had everything in common. Meanwhile, they conveniently ignore the many other verses that confirm the legitimacy of the faithful having their own resources.

Those who are living alternative sexual lifestyles present Jesus as the ultimate radical who challenged the status quo. According to them, the foes of Jesus were the judgmental religious leaders. These leaders were *exclusive*, while Jesus was *inclusive*, receiving all into community. Those who adhere to this worldview neglect to mention the fact that Jesus admonished sinners to repent (Luke 13:1-5). They also ignore the fact that Jesus' critique of the Pharisees was not that they were judgmental—but that they refused to believe the teachings of Moses:

- "Do not think that I will accuse you to the Father. There is one who accuses you: Moses, on whom you have set your hope. For if you believed Moses, you would believe me; for he wrote of me. But if you do not believe his writings, how will you believe my words?" (John 5:45-47)

Once again, a theology which is faithful to the Word of God seeks to reconcile verse with verse in order to understand Scripture in a coherent and unified way. There is far too much exegesis, or interpretation, of the Word which is done for the sole purpose of trying to reconcile Scripture with the norms of the prevailing culture.

For a good case in point, theistic evolutionists claim that there is no conflict between Scripture and evolution. They argue that it is impossible for these two sources of knowledge to conflict because they are focused on two entirely different areas. Evolution's concern is the physical world, while the Bible's focus is on the spiritual world. Conflict resolved!

However, the Bible teaches a great deal about the physical world. And many of those teachings are contrary to the claims of evolution. God speaking the world into existence and the introduction of sin and death into the world through Adam and Eve are two prime examples.

How can those who espouse theistic evolution declare that the Bible speaks only of the spiritual world? Theistic evolutionists answer by pointing out that, even though the Bible does address the physical world, its main concern is spiritual—as if it were possible to completely separate the two realms. They would also be quick to claim that the Bible speaks wrongly about the physical world because it reflects the errant cosmology of the Ancient Near East. Here is an example of how theistic evolutionists use the words of Scripture to denigrate what the Bible teaches about the physical world:

- …Yes, the world is established; it shall never be moved. (Psalm 93:1c)

How is it that the world will never be moved? Theistic evolutionists claim that the psalmist who wrote these words adhered to the same erroneous conviction as the rest of the ancient world—that the earth could not possibly be moved because it sits on a huge pedestal!

However, these same scholars ignore the fact that Scripture also declares that the righteous shall not be moved. How is that to be explained? Are the righteous also ensconced on a pedestal? Of course not. The righteous will not be "moved" in

25

the sense that they will not be destroyed. And so it is with the proper understanding of Psalm 93:1—*the earth will not be destroyed!*

Theistic evolutionists, as well as many others, try to manipulate and coerce Scripture into agreeing with whatever they happen to believe. This is exactly what I did when I first became a Christian, but I have learned my lesson. I have been so chastened that all I want is God's unadulterated truth. Because of the many painful experiences I have lived through, I need to know for certain that I am walking in His light and not my own perception of it.

Interpretation, therefore, is not simply a mental exercise. If that were the case, then we could learn wisdom from a book. However, wisdom is a gift from God, and it comes through humbling circumstances:

- The ear that listens to life-giving reproof will dwell among the wise. Whoever ignores instruction despises himself, but he who listens to reproof gains intelligence. The fear of the LORD is instruction in wisdom, and humility comes before honor. (Proverbs 15:31-33)

Who will listen to reproof? Who will solicit criticism? Only the one who has been humbled. Only the one who has come to despair of his own judgments and inclinations. This is the one who is ready for the "fear of the Lord." This is the one who is truly open to God's wisdom and correction.

I had willfully ignored instruction, thinking that I had all the right answers. The Lord disciplined me according to my own foolishness, allowing me to reap the consequences of my arrogance. He humbled me in order to lift me up. King David had confessed:

- It is good for me that I was afflicted, that I might learn your statutes. The law of your mouth is better to me than thousands of gold and silver pieces. (Psalm 119:71-72)

When we are afflicted, we will grab any life-preserver thrown our way. The Word was given to me, and now I value it more than anything else in my life. Therefore, I meditate on it continually, as the Lord instructed Joshua:

- "This Book of the Law shall not depart from your mouth, but you shall meditate on it day and night, so that you may be careful to do according to all that is written in it. For then you will make your way prosperous, and then you will have good success." (Joshua 1:8)

How do we understand this "Book of the Law," the Bible? Once again, it is not just a mental activity. Theology must be done on our knees. In order for us to have wisdom to properly understand His Word, we must cry out to the Lord. And He is well able to provide what we need:

- He said to them, "This is what I told you while I was still with you: Everything must be fulfilled that is written about me in the Law of Moses, the Prophets and the Psalms." *Then he opened their minds so they could understand the Scriptures.* (Luke 24:44-45, emphasis added)

Since the Lord can open our minds to understand His truths, we must be in prayer so that His plans and purposes are not overshadowed by our own interests and agendas.

Chapter 3

INTERPRETING SCRIPTURE ACCURATELY

CHAPTER SUMMARY

The way the world reacts to the fruit of our lives lived in faith is one means by which we might know that we are interpreting Scripture accurately.

How do we know when we have the right interpretation of Scripture? Actually, there are many ways we can know. I will concentrate here on just one of them.

According to the Book of James, the correct interpretation of God's Word bears good fruit:

- But the wisdom from above is first pure, then peaceable, gentle, open to reason, full of mercy and good fruits, impartial and sincere. And a harvest of righteousness is sown in peace by those who make peace. (James 3:17-18)

Our good fruit shows off the wisdom of God to the world. When our interpretation of Scripture guides us to live wisely and morally in the eyes of the world, this is a good indication that we have the proper understanding of God's Word.

Israel's godly influence upon her neighbors was most definitely a demonstration of the wisdom of God in their lives. After all, Moses had taught the Israelites that if they would live according to His laws, they would reveal God's wisdom to the nations around them:

- "See, I have taught you statutes and rules, as the LORD my God commanded me, that you should do them in the land that you are entering to take possession of it. Keep them and do them, for that will be your wisdom and your understanding in the sight of the peoples, who, when they hear all these statutes, will say, 'Surely this great nation is a wise and understanding people.' For what great nation is there that has a god so near to it as the LORD our God is to us, whenever we call upon him? And what great nation is there, that has statutes and rules so righteous as all this law that I set before you today?" (Deuteronomy 4:5-8)

By living out God's truths as He intended for them to be understood and practiced, Israel would be a light to the nations.

This same guiding principle pertains to us today. When we interpret and apply the Word accurately, our conduct will show forth God's wisdom and put our oppressors to shame:

- Keep your conduct among the Gentiles honorable, so that when they speak against you as evildoers, they may see your good deeds and glorify God on the day of visitation...For this is the will of God, that by doing good you should put to silence the ignorance of foolish people. (1 Peter 2:12, 15; see also Titus 2:5-10)

These teachings reflect the unassailable fact that, not only Christians but non-Christians alike, have the moral laws of God written on their hearts (Romans 2:14-15). Therefore, it is certain that those who do not know Christ do indeed know what is good and what is not. Even if they walk in the darkness of evil, they still know what is morally right. That is why, even if they hate the light of God's wisdom, they can only deny it with great difficulty.

However, if the way that believers interpret Scripture causes unbelievers to dismiss our faith, then perhaps we have failed to show God's wisdom in our understanding of what the Word is saying.

For example, many Christians have misinterpreted Jesus' teaching on "turning the other cheek" found in Luke 6:29. Some feel so confident in their literal understanding of what Jesus said that they would even refuse to report a burglary.

How do we know conclusively that such a response is wrong? The answer is simple and makes so much common sense: Any interpretation of the Word is wrong if it leads one to respond in a way that would bring disrepute upon the faith and upon the Church.

What if my sister is raped and I know the identity of the rapist? But, because of my horribly misguided understanding of what it means to "turn the other cheek," I do not bring charges against the perpetrator. Then, when my neighbor's wife is raped by the same man, her husband learns that I had refused to bring charges. He has every right to regard me—and my faith—with contempt.

This should teach us an essential lesson. If our interpretation of Scripture fails to reveal the wisdom of God, it is likely that we have the wrong interpretation.

If we speak and act according to God's wise teachings, we will be blessed; and we will have the opportunity to bless others, as well:

- Whoever despises the word brings destruction on himself, but he who reveres the commandment will be rewarded. The teaching of the wise is a fountain of life, that one may turn away from the snares of death. Good sense wins favor. (Proverbs 13:13-15)

When we live this way, it is highly likely that we are correctly interpreting Scripture and walking in the truth of His Word. And, as Proverbs 13 declares, we will win favor.

However, it is important for us to remember as well what Jesus so clearly taught: If we faithfully bear forth the light of Scripture, just as the world hated Jesus, so the world will hate us.

- "If the world hates you, know that it has hated me before it hated you. If you were of the world, the world would love you as its own; but because you are not of the world, but I chose you out of the world, therefore the world hates you. Remember the word that I said to you: 'A servant is not greater than his master.' If they persecuted me, they will also persecute you. If they kept my word, they will also keep yours." (John 15:18-20)

How do we reconcile these two very different Scriptural teachings? On the one hand, we will be rewarded and favored; on the other hand, the world will hate us. I think that there are two ways to understand these seemingly contradictory messages. For one thing, I think all of us are well aware that people are walking, breathing contradictions. They might truly hate us and yet still recognize our goodness.

The other possibility is this: Those who are hardened to the truth will hate us, while those who are being drawn to the light will hold us in esteem:

- But thanks be to God, who in Christ always leads us in triumphal procession, and through us spreads the fragrance of the knowledge of him everywhere. For we are the aroma of Christ to God among those who are being saved and among those who are perishing, to one a fragrance from death to death, to the other a fragrance from life to life...(2 Corinthians 2:14-16a)

Some will hate us…and some will love us.

Here is one last thought about how to know if we are interpreting Scripture accurately. Interpretation is like doing a puzzle. We know that the last piece of the puzzle belongs where it does because it fits in with all the other pieces. In the same way, the interpretation of a single verse must agree with all the other "pieces" of the biblical puzzle, if that interpretation is to be accurate.

Of course, it is not always as easy as that. The pieces of a puzzle are made to fit correctly into certain positions according to the various openings in the rest of the puzzle. However, sometimes our interpretations and theological conclusions are much more tenuous.

Why is that true? For one thing, in this life we are able to see only in part, like a poor reflection in a mirror (Deuteronomy 29:29; 1 Corinthians 8:2; 13:9-12). God has hidden much from us, perhaps because we are not yet ready to know certain things:

- It is the glory of God to conceal a matter…(Proverbs 25:2a)

For another thing, Scripture is infinitely deeper than the created world, of which we are but a part. Therefore once again, in this life, we will always be dependent upon God for any wisdom we might hope to possess:

- If any of you lacks wisdom, he should ask God, who gives generously to all without finding fault, and it will be given to him. (James 1:5)

This is most certainly as it should be. In this life and in the next, we are totally dependent on God for wisdom and, in fact, everything we need. What a great journey of faith we are on!

Chapter 4

UNDERSTANDING SCRIPTURE AS HISTORY

CHAPTER SUMMARY

How should we understand books like Jonah and Job? Are they history or allegory? Are the creation accounts and Noah's flood historical? In order to answer these questions, we must compare Scripture with Scripture. If the New Testament regards these books and accounts as history, then so must we.

Is the Bible historical or is it spiritual allegory? Of course, parts of the Bible are history, while other parts are not. So then, how can we determine the historical from the non-historical? If we take the Bible seriously, we should try to determine how the Bible itself regards its various writings. We compare Scripture with Scripture.

Let's start with the Book of Jonah. Is it historical? Did a fish actually swallow Jonah and vomit him up on a beach after three days? One way we can answer these questions is to see how Jesus answered them. Evidently, Jesus regarded Jonah as history:

- He answered, "A wicked and adulterous generation asks for a miraculous sign! But none will be given it except the sign of the prophet Jonah. For as Jonah was three days and three nights in the belly of a huge fish, so the Son of Man will be three days and three nights in the heart of the earth. The men of Nineveh will stand up at the judgment with this generation and condemn it; for they repented at the preaching of Jonah, and now one greater than Jonah is here." (Matthew 12:39-41; see also Matthew 16:4; Luke 11:29-30)

From His own words, it does not seem even remotely possible that Jesus could have understood the Book of Jonah as an allegory. If Jesus did not believe that Jonah had actually spent three days in the belly of a fish, then why would He declare that He was going to spend three days "in the heart of the earth"? There would be no basis for His comparison of Jonah's experience with what would soon be His own. If Jesus thought that the story of Jonah was an allegory, then He would be suggesting here that His three days in the grave would also be an allegory. Impossible!

Besides this, Jesus does not say, "*According to the tale*, Jonah was three days and three nights in the belly of a huge fish." Instead, He speaks as if this amazing thing actually happened.

In the same passage, Jesus also prophesied that "Nineveh will stand up at the judgment" of the Israelites of that generation. If it had been common knowledge that Jonah was simply a parable or an allegory, those who heard what Jesus had said would have scorned His words. After all, if the repentance of Nineveh was fictional, then how could anyone believe that the Ninevites would "stand up at the judgment" of Israel? However, Jesus was not scorned for what He said. The Israelites knew that the story of Jonah was historical.

❖ ❖ ❖

If we are followers of Christ, then we must follow Him also in the way that He thought and reasoned. According to Matthew 5:16-18, Jesus considered Scripture to be the undefiled Word of God and submitted to it in all regards. Quoting from Deuteronomy 8, He responded to Satan:

- "Man does not live on bread alone, but on *every word that comes from the mouth of God*." (Matthew 4:4, emphasis added)

This means that we too must live by "every word" of God and endeavor to understand the Scriptures as Jesus did. If He—as well as the Apostles—regarded the first several chapters of Genesis as history, then we too are constrained to regard those chapters in the same way.

Jesus based His teaching on marriage and divorce on the historicity of Genesis 1 and 2:

- "Haven't you read," he replied, "that at the beginning the Creator 'made them male and female' [Genesis 1:26-27] and said, 'For this reason a man will leave his father and mother and be united to his wife, and the two will become one flesh' [Genesis 2:24]? So they are no longer two, but one. Therefore what God has joined together, let man not separate." (Matthew 19:4-6)

Jesus' entire argument is based upon the history of God's work—how He created the first man and woman, made them one flesh and "joined [them] together."

If God had only *figuratively*—not historically—created and then joined Adam and Eve together, then we would have every right to *actually* divorce as long as we would not *figuratively* divorce. One who is contemplating divorce could reason that, "I will divorce my wife but remain married to her figuratively, in my heart." Of course, this is absurd. But what makes it so absurd is the absurd notion of a non-historical understanding of Jesus' words! Our Lord's clear intent in this passage was to demonstrate that divorce is wrong and that the Pharisees were wrong for trying to justify it.

Jesus built His case on the common understanding that Genesis is history. If Genesis had not been widely regarded as historical, the Pharisees could easily have retorted, "Well, God didn't *actually* join together Adam and Eve, so we are not prohibited from divorcing our wives." If Genesis is not history, then Jesus' argument would have completely collapsed.

This is not to deny that Genesis 1 and 2 are difficult to interpret. However, if we start with the assumption that these chapters are not historical, or that Jesus' understanding should not guide our understanding—Scripture interpreting Scripture—then we are dismissing our most important interpretive guidelines and constraints. Operating with this sort of invalid interpretive "freedom," the door is wide open to almost any interpretation of Genesis that anyone might choose to entertain.

❖ ❖ ❖

Did Paul regard these chapters of Genesis as historical, even though we find there a mix of poetry and theology? Absolutely. It is clear that the Apostle Paul understood that Adam was actually and historically created, first; and that it was the woman who had been deceived:

- For Adam was formed first, then Eve. And Adam was not the one deceived; it was the woman who was deceived and became a sinner. (1 Timothy 2:13-14, referring to Genesis 3 as history)

Paul also taught that Jesus was the second Adam:

- So it is written: "The first man Adam became a living being"; the last Adam, a life-giving spirit. The spiritual did not come first, but the natural, and after that the spiritual. The first man was of the dust of the earth, the second man from heaven. (1 Corinthians 15:45-47)

If Adam is a myth, then one could make a strong case that Christ also is a myth.

How important is it for us to know that Genesis teaches history? Not only is this question critical to interpretation, it is also critical to theology. The fact is, history and theology are inseparable. If we take away history, then we also take away the theology that is based upon it. If Jesus had not historically died on the Cross, there would be no theology of the Cross. And if there were no theology of the Cross, there could be no redemption. If Adam and Eve had not actually rebelled against God—causing the fall—then we would need to blame some sort of evolutionary understanding of creation for the problems of mankind. Such a point of view undermines the theology of the entire Bible.

Speaking of evolution, theistic evolutionists claim that it is only because they have been able to "reconcile" evolution with the Bible that many educated Christians have remained in the Church. However, this suggests that God prefers a watered-down faith to no faith at all. Such a shoddy, error-laden perspective reminds us of the Spirit's letter to the church at Laodicea:

- "'I know your works: you are neither cold nor hot. Would that you were either cold or hot! So, because you are lukewarm, and neither hot nor cold, I will spit you out of my mouth. For you say, I am rich, I have prospered, and I need nothing, not realizing that you are wretched, pitiable, poor, blind, and naked." (Revelation 3:15-17)

❖ ❖ ❖

Is the Book of Job purely allegorical/figurative or is it also historical?

Once again, to answer this question, we need to see what the Bible itself has to say about it. When we examine the Scriptures, we find that the Bible regards the Book of Job as history:

- The word of the LORD came to me: "Son of man, if a country sins against me by being unfaithful and I stretch out my hand against it to cut off its food supply and send famine upon it and kill its men and their animals, even if these three men—Noah, Daniel and Job—were in it, they could save only themselves by their righteousness," declares the Sovereign LORD. (Ezekiel 14:12-14)

Thus, we can clearly see that God regarded Job as an actual, historical person—the same as Daniel and Noah.

James also regarded him as historical:

- As you know, we consider blessed those who have persevered. You have heard of Job's perseverance and have seen what the Lord finally brought about. The Lord is full of compassion and mercy. (James 5:11)

James understood that God's mercy to Job was a clear demonstration of the fact that "The Lord is full of compassion and mercy." If the Book of Job had not been a matter of history, then the words of God through James would not have provided valid evidence for the mercy of God. And besides, allegories— when properly understood—do not provide evidence, but merely illustration.

❖ ❖ ❖

What about the historicity of a worldwide flood destroying all mankind except for Noah and his family?

The Genesis account and the subsequent commentary bear all the signs of actual history:

- The waters prevailed above the mountains, covering them fifteen cubits deep. And all flesh died that moved on the earth, birds, livestock, beasts, all swarming creatures that swarm on the earth, and all mankind. Everything on the dry land in whose nostrils was the breath of life died. He blotted out every living thing that was on the face of the ground, man and animals and creeping things and birds of the heavens. They were blotted out from the earth. Only Noah was left, and those who were with him in the ark. (Genesis 7:20-23)

How does the rest of the Bible regard the historicity of this account? We have already seen that Ezekiel regarded Noah as a real person. As it turns out, Jesus also regarded the account of the worldwide flood as history:

- "For as were the days of Noah, so will be the coming of the Son of Man. For as in those days before the flood they were eating and drinking, marrying and giving in marriage, until the day when Noah entered the ark, and they were unaware until the flood came and swept them all away, so will be the coming of the Son of Man." (Matthew 24:37-39)

If the Bible's account of Noah is merely allegorical, then how are we to view the return of the Son of Man, Jesus? Is that also to be understood as no more than an illustrative story?

The Book of Hebrews also regards Noah and the flood as history:

- By faith Noah, being warned by God concerning events as yet unseen, in reverent fear constructed an ark for the saving of his household. By this he condemned the world and became an heir of the righteousness that comes by faith. (Hebrews 11:7)

Thus, we can see that Hebrews upholds Noah as an exemplar of the faith. If the biblical record of the flood was just a myth, there is no way that Noah would be honored in Hebrews 11 along with Moses, the patriarchs and many others.

Peter as well invokes Noah and the flood as history. He uses the account of Noah to build a theology to prove that God's promise of a future judgment is to be taken seriously:

- For if God did not spare angels when they sinned, but cast them into hell and committed them to chains of gloomy darkness to be kept until the judgment; if he did not spare the ancient world, but preserved Noah, a herald of righteousness, with seven others, when he brought a flood upon the world of the ungodly...(2 Peter 2:4-5)

If the examples that Peter used here had not been actual and historical events but rather myths, his reasoning would have fallen apart. If these events were merely fables, then God's future judgment should also be dismissed as nothing more than a fiction. However, Peter clearly believed that these events actually took place. That is the only way that he was able to conclude his line of reasoning the way he did:

- ...then the Lord knows how to rescue the godly from trials, and to keep the unrighteous under punishment until the day of judgment...(2 Peter 2:9)

Peter could not possibly have drawn such a conclusion from a myth or a fable.

A historical, worldwide flood teaches several important theological truths:

1. God judges.

2. God rescues those who are His.

3. We must become reconciled to Him and not become enamored with philosophies that offer only their own base-less varieties of hope.

❖ ❖ ❖

We are keenly aware that the Bible's theology is distasteful and unappealing to modern ears. A God of judgment? A God who actually judges sin? Such a God is antithetical to the spirit of our age. And sadly, this mind-set has infiltrated the Church. Many in the Church today assuage their conscience concerning these politically incorrect biblical accounts by consoling themselves with the belief that these stories are just myths. A loving God would never do such things to His creation.

However, if we truly open our eyes and study human history, we would have to acknowledge that our omnipotent, omniscient and—yes, loving God—allows all manner of horrors to occur.

Let us therefore humble ourselves before the God of the Bible and walk in His light

Chapter 5

UNDERSTANDING THE OMNISCIENCE OF GOD

CHAPTER SUMMARY

There are some verses that make it seem as if God does not know the future. However, this seeming conundrum might be a by-product of the way that God inspired the use of anthropomorphic—man-centered—language.

Is God omniscient? If He is, then there is no reason for Him to change His mind, since He already knows everything.

The issue of God's omniscience impacts us directly. It means that God already knows us completely. This also means that He will not turn away from us or revise His promises to us because of changes we might go through during the course of our lives. There are many verses that explicitly inform us that God is perfect in His knowledge of all things, including every day of our lives:

- You discern my going out and my lying down; you are familiar with all my ways. Before a word is on my tongue you know it completely, O LORD. (Psalm 139:3-4)

- Nothing in all creation is hidden from God's sight. Everything is uncovered and laid bare before the eyes of him to whom we must give account. (Hebrews 4:13)

So, it is clear—Scripture supports the idea of God's omniscience. But are events that have not yet happened "hidden from God's sight"? Evidently not:

- Great is our Lord and mighty in power; his understanding has no limit. (Psalm 147:5)

If His understanding has no limit, then it follows that His knowledge of the future would also have no limit.

- "See, the former things have taken place, and new things I declare; before they spring into being I announce them to you." (Isaiah 42:9)

- "Who then is like me? Let him proclaim it. Let him declare and lay out before me what has happened since I established my ancient people, and what is yet to come—yes, let him foretell what will come." (Isaiah 44:7)

The Lord is declaring here that there is no one like Him. No one besides Him is able to declare "what is yet to come":

- "I make known the end from the beginning, from ancient times, what is still to come. I say: My purpose will stand, and I will do all that I please." (Isaiah 46:10)

It does not seem as if there are any details about things yet to come that He does not know:

- "For I knew how stubborn you were; the sinews of your neck were iron, your forehead was bronze. Therefore I told you these things long ago; before they happened I announced them to you so that you could not say, 'My idols did them; my wooden image and metal god ordained them.'" (Isaiah 48:4-5)

God allows no room for any idols to fill in the so-called missing links about what He knows of the future.

To summarize the last few paragraphs: As far as foreknowledge is concerned, God is not even slightly myopic—He is omniscient!

❖ ❖ ❖

However, there are a number of verses that also seem to suggest that God is not perfect in what He knows of the future. For example, shortly before the Israelites entered the Promised Land, God gave Moses a song so that he could teach it to Israel. In this song, besides a prophecy about Israel's future rebellion, there is also this curious detail:

- "I will hide my face from them," he said, "*and see what their end will be;* for they are a perverse generation, children who are unfaithful." (Deuteronomy 32:20, emphasis added)

This verse suggests that God does not know what is going to happen to Israel. He will have to play a cosmic version of "wait and see." And yet, when we read the lyrics to the rest of the song, we find out that God knows precisely what is going to happen to His people:

- "I will heap calamities upon them and spend my arrows against them. I will send wasting famine against them, consuming pestilence and deadly plague; I will send against them the fangs of wild beasts, the venom of vipers that glide in the dust." (Deuteronomy 32:23-24)

A few verses later, we see this:

- Rejoice, O nations, with his people, for he will avenge the blood of his servants; he will take vengeance on his enemies and make atonement for his land and people. (Deuteronomy 32:43)

44

How then do we explain what some might consider to be a contradiction in these two verses? Does God know everything, including the future—or does He not?

Perhaps God is merely using language as a man or woman might, as if to say: "My words will be vindicated when what I have said comes to pass." Or, perhaps He is simply saying "We shall see...", as we have all said at some point, even though we know what will happen. When we look at Deuteronomy 32:20 in this light, then the verse makes good sense. Let's look at this verse one more time with our new understanding:

- "I will hide my face from them," he said, "*and see what their end will be; for they are a perverse generation, children who are unfaithful.*" (Deuteronomy 32:20, emphasis added)

The conundrum is resolved.

❖ ❖ ❖

Some verses of Scripture suggest that there were occasions when God seemed to change His mind. For example, let us consider what God said to the prophet Samuel concerning Israel's first king:

- "It repenteth me that I have set up Saul to be king: for he is turned back from following me, and hath not performed my commandments." And it grieved Samuel; and he cried unto the LORD all night. (1 Samuel 15:11)

The King James Version makes it seem as if God had changed His mind about Saul, based on new information He had learned. However, in the same chapter, Samuel declares emphatically that God does not change His mind:

- Samuel said to him [Saul], "The LORD has torn the kingdom of Israel from you today and has given it to one of your neighbors—to one better than you. *He who is the Glory of Israel does not lie or change his mind* ["repent" in the KJV]; for he is not a man, that he should change his mind." (1 Samuel 15:28-29, emphasis added)

So, in this verse, Samuel says that God does not change His mind. Yet, referring back to v. 11, it says that God does repent, or change His mind. The same Hebrew word is used in both sets of verses. How do we reconcile this apparent contradiction?

In the Bible, words are often used differently, on different occasions. In regard to v. 11, the NIV translates the Hebrew as, "I [God] am grieved that I have made Saul king..." This is not to say that He had changed His mind, but only the course of action according to His plan. And His plan, as set forth in the Scriptures, was that the lineage of the kings of Israel would come only through the tribe of Judah, and not Benjamin, the tribe of Saul:

- "The scepter will not depart from Judah, nor the ruler's staff from between his feet, until he comes to whom it belongs and the obedience of the nations is his." (Genesis 49:10)

God's perfect omniscience is not just an academic matter. It is a concern as important as our food—our peace, our trust, and our sense of well-being. If God is not omniscient, and if He therefore might change His mind towards us at any time, then we have no basis for genuine peace. At some point He might decide to change the promises He made towards us. He might even decide that He no longer wants to have us for His own. It would be impossible to have any sort of joyful confidence in such a God. And finally, how could we have any assurance about our salvation or even our place in heaven, if God acted in such a capricious way?

The study of physics—based on the order and pattern with which God created the natural world—assures us that God is not in the business of learning new facts and arbitrarily changing His mind. Instead, as far as we can tell, the laws of physics remain immutable, elegant, and universal. And so it is with God—whose masterful ordering of the universe is the foundation for the laws of physics. God has given us no hint at all that He is second-guessing Himself as new information comes into His "lab."

It has been alleged by some that God had no idea how Abraham would respond to His directive concerning the sacrifice of Isaac. Would God be able to fulfill His covenant through Abraham? As far as these folks are concerned, God did not know. According to the Genesis account, as Abraham was getting ready to plunge the knife into his son, the Angel of the LORD intervened:

- "Do not lay a hand on the boy," he said. "Do not do anything to him. *Now I know that you fear God*, because you have not withheld from me your son, your only son." (Genesis 22:12, emphasis added)

The Angel of the LORD then renewed the covenant with Abraham. It seems unlikely that the Lord did not know the outcome of this trial. For one thing, Genesis 12:1-3 declares that God had previously made an unconditional promise to Abraham that he would be a blessing to the entire world. In addition, at a later point in the story, the Lord had indicated that Abraham's obedience was a foregone conclusion:

- Then the LORD said, "Shall I hide from Abraham what I am about to do? *Abraham will surely become a great and powerful nation, and all nations on earth will be blessed through him.* For I have chosen ["known" in the Hebrew] him, so that he will direct his children and his household after him to keep the way of the LORD by doing what is right and just, so that the LORD will bring about for Abraham what he has promised him." (Genesis 18:17-19, emphasis added)

Abraham's future obedience was clearly known by the Lord before-hand. And thus He knew as well that His covenant would most assuredly be fulfilled through this "friend of God."

How then are we to understand God saying, "Now I know"? Did He not know before? Perhaps we can make sense of these words if we look at them like this: "Now I know *with my eyes.*"

In any event, God's foreknowledge is one of the foundation stones upon which the entire biblical revelation rests. Everything that He has promised depends upon His perfect knowledge and ordaining of the future.

❖ ❖ ❖

God often expresses Himself in anthropomorphic language—language that we humans understand and use and with which we are familiar. Here is a good example of how God sometimes uses this manner of speech to communicate. After the flood, God promised Noah that He would remember His covenant:

- "Whenever I bring clouds over the earth and the rainbow appears in the clouds, *I will remember my covenant* between me and you and all living creatures of every kind. Never again will the waters become a flood to destroy all life." (Genesis 9:14-15, emphasis added; see also Leviticus 26:42, 45; Ezekiel 16:60)

Even those who deny that God knows the future acknowledge that this passage does not suggest that He had temporarily forgotten His covenant with Noah. Nor do these verses suggest that He had to make an effort to recall what was no longer in His mind. In view of the many verses that proclaim that God's knowledge is perfect, we must interpret this saying as simply another example of God's attempt to speak to us in language that we can understand.

Our Father in heaven knows ALL things—He is omniscient. Of course, the Son knew this as well. Jesus assured His followers that—unlike unbelievers—there was no need for them to worry about their needs. God knew what they needed even before they could verbalize their requests:

- "Do not be like them, for your Father knows what you need before you ask him." (Matthew 6:8)

God knows all things!

Here is yet another foundational and comforting truth about God's knowledge: The Bible assures us that—according to 2 Timothy 2:19—"The Lord knows those who are His." We can take the blessing of this wonderful truth to the bank, as they say. Furthermore, nothing in all of creation will be able to separate us from Him (Romans 8:38-39). But let us remember that, in order to give us this—or any—assurance, He must have perfect foreknowledge. Without a perfect knowledge of all things, including the future, He would always be learning new things. And with this new knowledge, there would always be the likelihood that He would have to revise His plans and renege on the promises He has made to us.

Once again, we who are His can rest assured…God knows all things!

❖ ❖ ❖

A Philosophical Challenge to God's Foreknowledge

It has been claimed that if God is omniscient—if He has perfect foreknowledge—then human beings have no freewill. After all, if God knows how we will act, then it follows that we must act according to His foreknowledge. Therefore, according to this line of reasoning, we cannot have freewill.

Here is this theory in logical form:

1. If God has perfect foreknowledge, *the future must happen the way that God knew it would happen* even before He created the world.

2. Therefore, the only choice we will make is the one that He foreknew that we *would* make.

3. CONCLUSION: Since we will not act otherwise, we lack freewill.

However, the conclusion does not follow logically from the premises. As a Christian, I accept premise #1 and #2. But I do not believe that the second part of the conclusion logically follows the premises:

For example, I know what my wife will do when she feels dirty. She will take a shower. Does this mean that she has no freewill? My foreknowledge about what she would do does not mean that she did not make a freewill choice to take a shower.

Although I *will* act as God foreknows I will act, it does not follow that I *could not* act otherwise. I could have acted otherwise, but I simply chose not to, as God foreknew. Therefore, God is perfectly omniscient...and I am free to choose!

Chapter 6

UNDERSTANDING THE TORAH CHRISTOLOGICALLY

CHAPTER SUMMARY
There are glimpses of Christ and His Cross throughout the Pentateuch, the Five Books of Moses.

Do the Five Books of Moses—also known as the Torah, or the Pentateuch—mention Jesus? I have been asked this question on several occasions. Although Jesus is not mentioned by name, there is quite an impressive collection of His portraits hanging in each of the Five Books.

In the pages of the Hebrew Scriptures, the visible, pre-incarnate appearances of Christ are called Christophanies, or theophanies. "The Angel of the LORD" is the phrase most closely associated with these appearances. There is evidence that this "Angel" is actually God the Son. Let's take a look at the first manifestation of this mysterious Angel when He appears to Hagar, Abraham's concubine and the mother of Ishmael:

- The angel of the LORD found her by a spring of water in the wilderness, the spring on the way to Shur. And he said, "Hagar, servant of Sarai, where have you come from and where are you going?" She said, "I am fleeing from my mistress Sarai." The angel of the LORD said to her, "Return to your mistress and submit to her." The angel of the LORD also said to her, "I will surely multiply your offspring so that they cannot be numbered for multitude." And the angel of the LORD said to her, "Behold, you are pregnant and shall bear a son. You shall call his name Ishmael, because the LORD has listened to your affliction. He shall be a wild donkey of a man, his hand against everyone and everyone's hand against him, and he shall dwell over against all his kinsmen." So she called the name of the LORD who spoke to her, "You are a God of seeing," for she said, "Truly here I have seen him who looks after me." (Genesis 16:7-13)

This narrative claims that it was the LORD—Yahweh—who spoke to Hagar. Hagar claimed as well that she had seen God, revealed to her in the person of the Angel of the LORD. Two chapters later:

- The LORD [Yahweh] appeared to him [Abraham] by the oaks of Mamre, as he sat at the door of his tent in the heat of the day. (Genesis 18:1)

Please note that, according to Exodus 33:20, Yahweh—the Father—appears to no one. Therefore, this appearance must have been a Christophany of Yahweh, the Son.

Returning to the Genesis 18 account, we see that the angels who were accompanying Yahweh began to make their way toward Sodom. But Abraham drew near to the LORD and interceded for the city. After their conversation:

- The LORD ["Yahweh," the Son] went his way, when he had finished speaking to Abraham, and Abraham returned to his place. (Genesis 18:33)

Many years later, Abraham's grandson Jacob wrestled all night with a "man." Jacob soon realized that this man was actually God:

- So Jacob called the name of the place Peniel, saying, "For I have seen God face to face, and yet my life has been delivered." (Genesis 32:30)

At the end of his life, while he was blessing the sons of Joseph, Jacob identified God as the "Angel" with whom he had wrestled so many years before:

- And he [Jacob] blessed Joseph and said, "The God before whom my fathers Abraham and Isaac walked, the God who has been my shepherd all my life long to this day, the Angel who has redeemed me from all evil, bless the boys; and in them let my name be carried on, and the name of my fathers Abraham and Isaac; and let them grow into a multitude in the midst of the earth." (Genesis 48:15-16)

So, after Jacob had invoked "God" twice and "the Angel" a third time, he implored them—*in the singular*—to bless his family. Therefore, it is clear that Jacob understood that the Angel of the LORD was also God.

Here is yet another observation that confirms the identity of "the Angel of the LORD" as God: Jacob claimed that it was this Angel who had "redeemed me from all evil." We know that it is God who is clearly identified as the Redeemer (2 Samuel 4:9; Psalm 34:22; 121:7; Isaiah 44:22-23; 49:7). Therefore, "the Angel of the LORD" and God and the Redeemer are all referring to the same divine Person.

Much later, the prophet Isaiah wrote that the "Angel of His Presence" had saved and redeemed Israel:

- In all their affliction He was afflicted, and the Angel of His Presence saved them; in His love and in His pity He redeemed them; and He bore them and carried them all the days of old. (Isaiah 63:9)

Thus, it is plain to see that Isaiah also equated this Angel with God.

Let us not overlook one of the most famous theophanies, when the Angel appeared to Moses in the midst of a burning bush in the middle of the desert:

- And the angel of the LORD appeared to him in a flame of fire out of the midst of a bush. He looked, and behold, the bush was burning, yet it was not consumed. And Moses said, "I will turn aside to see this great sight, why the bush is not burned." When the LORD saw that he turned aside to see, God called to him out of the bush, "Moses, Moses!" And he said, "Here I am." (Exodus 3:2-4)

We should notice in these verses that this Angel is called both "LORD" and "God." All of these appearances provide us with incontrovertible evidence that God—or Yahweh—is not the single Person that the rabbis claim about the Godhead. As we have seen, the Son—manifest especially as "the Angel of the LORD"— appeared on a number of occasions. Furthermore, all of these references should put to rest the rabbinic claim that God does not take on human form. Instead, these appearances of a Messianic figure provide us with powerful evidence for the Trinity.

❖ ❖ ❖

The Angel of the LORD appears in many other places throughout the Pentateuch. He was the One who brought Israel out of Egypt:

- When we cried out to the Lord, He heard our voice and sent the Angel and brought us up out of Egypt… (Numbers 20:16a)

However, there are other verses that claim that it was the LORD who brought Israel out of Egypt:

- And the LORD went before them by day in a pillar of cloud to lead them along the way, and by night in a pillar of fire to give them light, that they might travel by day and by night. (Exodus 13:21; see also Deuteronomy 31:2-3)

How do we resolve this apparent contradiction? From Numbers 20:16, it is clear that the Angel Himself is God, and yet He seems to be presented in a very distinct way, and, as a very distinct Person. For if we examine the verse again, we can see that the Lord "...heard our voice and sent the Angel..."

In the following verses, we can see once again that God differentiated Himself from His Angel:

- "Behold, I send an Angel before you to keep you in the way and to bring you into the place which I have prepared. Beware of Him and obey His voice; do not provoke Him, for He will not pardon your transgressions; for My name is in Him." (Exodus 23:20-21)

When the Word declares that God's "name is in Him," this is the same as saying that God's essence, or nature, is in Him. This is more proof that God and the Angel are one—and yet they are distinct. In yet another verse, God the Father makes a sharp differentiation between Himself and the Divine Angel:

- "And I will send My Angel before you, and I will drive out the Canaanite and the Amorite and the Hittite and the Perizzite and the Hivite and the Jebusite. Go up to a land flowing with milk and honey; for I will not go up in your midst, lest I consume you on the way, for you are a stiff-necked people." (Exodus 33:2-3)

From this verse, we discover that God the Father could not be in the presence of Israel. Furthermore, Scripture proclaims that the Father can never be seen because He dwells in unapproachable light:

- …God, the blessed and only Ruler, the King of kings and Lord of lords, who alone is immortal and who lives in unapproachable light, whom no one has seen or can see. To him be honor and might forever. Amen. (I Timothy 6:15b-16)

In addition, we have these words from the Old Testament:

- But He said [to Moses], "You cannot see My face; for no man shall see Me, and live." (Exodus 33:20)

That is why God the Father sent His Angel to accompany Israel out of Egypt. Nevertheless, as it turned out, God indeed was seen:

- So the Lord spoke to Moses face to face, as a man speaks to his friend. (Exodus 33:11a)

How is it that God was seen and yet cannot be seen? This dilemma is resolved when we recognize that it must have been God the Son Who was seen, and not God the Father.

Let's take a look at another passage that demonstrates this truth. God had reprimanded Moses' sister and brother, who were attempting to usurp some of Moses' authority:

- And he said, "Hear my words: If there is a prophet among you, I the LORD make myself known to him in a vision; I speak with him in a dream. Not so with my servant Moses. He is faithful in all my house. With him I speak mouth to mouth, clearly, and not in riddles, and he beholds the form of the LORD. Why then were you not afraid to speak against my servant Moses?" (Numbers 12:6-8)

Again, this sounds like a contradiction. Either God cannot be seen...or Moses had actually seen Him. There is an explanation that makes perfect sense: Moses had actually seen God in the person of the Angel of the LORD, the second Person of the Trinity. In an awe-inspiring Christophany on Mt. Sinai, Moses had seen a pre-incarnate manifestation of Jesus Christ.

To back up this claim, there are other proofs. Stephen, before his martyrdom, also described the giving of the Law on Mt. Sinai as an encounter with the living Christ:

- "This is the one [Moses] who was in the congregation in the wilderness with the angel [of the LORD, or Christ] who spoke to him at Mount Sinai, and with our fathers..." (Acts 7:38a)

The Apostle Paul, writing about the same scene, claimed that Moses had encountered an "intermediary":

- Why then the law? It was added because of transgressions, until the offspring should come to whom the promise had been made, and it was put in place through angels by an intermediary. (Galatians 3:19; see also Hebrews 2:2)

This "intermediary" was the second Person of the Trinity, Jesus Christ.

What about the appearance of God in the Temple, portrayed to us in Isaiah 6?

- In the year that King Uzziah died, I saw the Lord seated on a throne, high and exalted, and the train of his robe filled the temple. (Isaiah 6:1-2)

Did Isaiah actually see God the Father? Not according to the Apostle John. He identifies the One Whom Isaiah saw as Jesus. In addition to the quotation from Isaiah 6, John quoted several other passages from Isaiah and then made this categorical statement:

- Isaiah said this because he saw Jesus' glory and spoke about him. (John 12:41)

Without an adequate understanding of the multiple Persons of the Godhead, there is no way to resolve some of these seeming paradoxes of Scripture. And yet, when these and similar verses are properly understood, they provide us with wonderful glimpses of the Trinity in the Torah.

❖ ❖ ❖

The rabbis and the various cults do not seem to want to engage this evidence; it simply does not accord with their worldview. However, the Christophanies I have mentioned here do not exhaust the Pentateuchal evidence.

Abraham had a mysterious encounter with a man named Melchizedek, whose name means "Righteous King." He is also variously described as the priest of the Most High God and the King of Salem—or "peace," in Hebrew. In his amazing meeting with Melchizedek, Abraham recognizes His authority and gives tithes to Him (Genesis 14:20; see also Psalm 110). In fact, Melchizedek seems to be more than human. We are told that he had no parents:

- He is without father or mother or genealogy, having neither beginning of days nor end of life, but resembling the Son of God he continues a priest forever. (Hebrews 7:3)

Only God has no beginning or end. Therefore, Abraham's experience with Melchizedek must have been a Christophany.

Judging from Abraham's subsequent actions, this encounter seems to have been transformative for the patriarch:

- After his [Abram's] return from the defeat of Chedorlaomer and the kings who were with him, the king of Sodom went out to meet him at the Valley of Shaveh (that is, the King's Valley). And Melchizedek king of Salem brought out bread and wine. (He was priest of God Most High.) And he blessed him and said, "Blessed be Abram by God Most High, Possessor of heaven and earth; and blessed be God Most High, who has delivered your enemies into your hand!" And Abram gave him a tenth of everything. (Genesis 14:17-20)

Why did Abram give Melchizedek a tenth of everything he had won in the rescue of Lot? Perhaps he did this because Melchizedek had just revealed to him that his victory over the marauders had been a gift from God. Then, we see that the generally conniving and cowardly Abraham—see Genesis 20—declared to the King of Sodom that he would take none of the plunder that had been won. What could have been the catalyst for all these signs of a major change of heart? Evidently, Abraham must have been convinced about the very special Personhood of the priest, Melchizedek.

In the next chapter, Genesis 15, Abraham seems to have had another Christophany, or divine encounter. Abraham had asked God to confirm His promises to him. God complied to the request with a covenant-making ceremony. In the forms of a blazing torch and a smoking firepot—symbols of wrath and judgment—He passed between the butchered parts of animals. In this intensely symbolic and visually striking way, God was pledging to honor the promises He had made to Abraham in the Covenant. He kept His Word to Abraham on the Cross—

through the wrath and judgment that He would allow to be released upon Himself.

God the Son was thus painting a self-portrait of His future suffering.

He would do this in other ways, as well. As the Son of a woman, Jesus would reverse the fall by crushing Satan, the malevolent force behind the serpent in the Garden of Eden. However, in the process, the "serpent" would strike His heel. Here is what God said to the serpent after Adam and Eve had sinned:

- "And I will put enmity between you and the woman, and between your offspring and hers; he will crush your head, and you will strike his heel." (Genesis 3:15).

Satan struck the heel of Christ on the Cross.

Abraham was asked to sacrifice his "only son" Isaac on Mt. Moriah. This was a foreshadowing of the way that God would give "His only begotten Son" on Calvary. However, before Abraham went through with the sacrifice, the Angel of the LORD intervened and provided a ram for an offering instead of Isaac:

- And the angel of the LORD called to Abraham a second time from heaven and said, "By myself I have sworn, declares the LORD, because you have done this and have not withheld your son, your only son, I will surely bless you…" (Genesis 22:15-17a)

Interestingly, Abraham understood far more about this encounter than might seem readily apparent. Instead of naming the mountain upon which he was to sacrifice Isaac, "God *has* provided," Abraham named it, "God *will* provide." This suggests that Abraham more than likely knew that God would one day provide another sacrifice on that very same mountain:

- So Abraham called the name of that place, "The LORD will provide"; as it is said to this day, "On the mount of the LORD it shall be provided." (Genesis 22:14)

And, just what would be provided? An offering similar to the one that Abraham had been asked to provide—a Father offering His Son. Perhaps Jesus was thinking of this milestone of the Hebrew Scriptures when He said:

- "Your father Abraham rejoiced that he would see my day. He saw it and was glad." (John 8:56)

What was it that Abraham saw? What exactly was Jesus' "day"? It was the day of His glory:

- And Jesus answered them, "The hour has come for the Son of Man to be glorified. Truly, truly, I say to you, unless a grain of wheat falls into the earth and dies, it remains alone; but if it dies, it bears much fruit." (John 12:23-24)

Why did Abraham rejoice to see Jesus' day? He understood that God the Father would, on that very day, offer His only-begotten Son. And His offering would not only be the substitute for Abraham's son, but for the sins of the entire world.

❖ ❖ ❖

As we have seen, God gave Israel many previews, or foreshadowings, of the Cross. He was always preaching the Gospel. Shortly after celebrating God's goodness in bringing them to safety through the sea, the Israelites rebelled against the Lord. They were so thirsty that they wanted to kill Moses for bringing them out of Egypt. He cried out to the Lord:

- And the LORD said unto Moses, Go on before the people, and take with thee of the elders of Israel; and thy rod, wherewith thou smotest the river, take in thine hand, and go. Behold, I will stand before thee there upon the rock in Horeb; and thou shalt smite the rock, and there shall come water out of it, that the people may drink. And Moses did so in the sight of the elders of Israel. (Exodus 17:5-6)

The Israelites wanted to indict God, and He was surprisingly ready to submit to their accusations. Moses was instructed to take his staff of judgment and, followed by the elders, walk through the midst of the people. The Israelites would have perceived—unmistakably—that Moses' actions were a sign that there was about to be a trial and an execution. However, instead of Israel being punished for their rebellion against God, He would be the One to suffer. God would "stand" on the rock as a defendant before Israel, and Moses would symbolically strike Him down with his staff. God would suffer the execution—which Israel deserved—while the Israelites would be blessed exceedingly from the most unlikely place. From a rock, life-giving waters would flow.

From the most unlikely place, this world would later be blessed. In the midst of the worst rebellion imaginable, Israel and the Gentiles would strike down the Savior of the world on a cross. Instead of the punishment for this most heinous of crimes falling upon the guilty, judgment would fall upon the innocent One. Those who were deserving of the ultimate chastisement would be blessed with living water (John 4:1-14).

❖ ❖ ❖

Here is another Gospel message from the pages of the Old Testament. In this account, the Israelites had yet again rebelled against the Lord. As a result, they were dying from poisonous snake bites.

- The LORD said to Moses, "Make a fiery serpent and set it on a pole, and everyone who is bitten, when he sees it, shall live." So Moses made a bronze serpent and set it on a pole. And if a serpent bit anyone, he would look at the bronze serpent and live. (Numbers 21:8-9)

Fifteen hundred years later, Jesus explained the symbolism:

- "And as Moses lifted up the serpent in the wilderness, so must the Son of Man be lifted up, that whoever believes in him may have eternal life." (John 3:14-15)

Israel received physical healing by looking at a sinful serpent that had been lifted up on a pole. We experience spiritual healing by looking to our Lord, Who became sin for us by being lifted up on another "pole." He did this so that we might become the righteousness of God (2 Corinthians 5:21).

❖ ❖ ❖

God sometimes uses the unlikeliest people to spread His Good News. For example, the Lord revealed King Jesus to a false prophet, Balaam. God had given him a series of astounding prophecies. According to Numbers 24:5, Balaam was enabled to see the loveliness of Israel's tents—though they were worn out. Even more impressive, Balaam was shown an Israel without any iniquity:

- "No misfortune is seen in Jacob, no misery observed in Israel. The LORD their God is with them; the shout of the King is among them." (Numbers 23:21)

How could this be? The King was in their midst!

After this, God again revealed to Balaam this mysterious King in the midst of Israel. Paradoxically, Balaam prophesied:

- "I see him, but not now; I behold him, but not near: a star shall come out of Jacob, and a scepter shall rise out of Israel." (Numbers 24:17; see also Genesis 49:10)

Israel's King was there, but He wasn't. He was present, but not in His fullness.

Much later—unwittingly—the Roman magistrate…

- …Pilate also wrote an inscription and put it on the cross. It read, "Jesus of Nazareth, the King of the Jews." (John 19:19)

However, this title troubled the chief priests:

- So the chief priests of the Jews said to Pilate, "Do not write, 'The King of the Jews,' but rather, 'This man said, I am King of the Jews.'" Pilate answered, "What I have written I have written." (John 19:21-22)

Interestingly, Jesus never called Himself "King of the Jews." Instead, Pilate seems to have been divinely led to write this. One evil man—Balaam—referring to a scepter that would rise out of Israel, had prophesied the coming King. Another evil man—Pilate—had highlighted the fulfillment of this prophecy. And the chief priests and rabbis who had been so troubled could do nothing to change what had been written…or what had been foreordained by God.

❖ ❖ ❖

Usually, when we think of Christ in the Pentateuch, we think of this prophecy of Moses:

- "The LORD your God will raise up for you a prophet like me from among you, from your brothers—it is to him you shall listen… 'I will raise up for them a prophet like you from among their brothers. And I will put my words in his mouth, and he shall speak to them all that I command him. And whoever will not listen to my words that he shall speak in my name, I myself will require it of him.'" (Deuteronomy 18:15, 18-19; see also Exodus 23:20-23)

Yet, we must not overlook one last portrait of our Savior. Before the Israelites went in to the Promised Land, God gave Moses a song so that he could teach them about their future. Here are the last few lines:

- Rejoice, O nations, with his people, for he will avenge the blood of his servants; he will take vengeance on his enemies *and make atonement for his land and people.* (Deuteronomy 32:43, emphasis added)

How strange—God Himself would make atonement! What about the Levites, the priests? Why did He not appoint them to make atonement through the sacrificial system? The answer is profound: Only God could provide a truly adequate atonement. Only God could make a satisfactory payment for the sins of the world, a payment that the blood of animals would never have been able to provide.

So now we understand. Jesus has revealed Himself throughout the Pentateuch, all the books of Moses…preaching His Good News to all who have the eyes to see and the ears to hear.

Chapter 7

UNDERSTANDING THE BOOK OF RUTH

CHAPTER SUMMARY

Naomi had lost everything and was crushed. However, her brokenness was only a prelude to the revelation of God's surpassing, surprising grace.

The sweetest blessings are often the ones far beyond our reach—blessings that seem unattainable, the blessings for which we must wait the longest. The Book of Ruth is a book of delayed and completely unexpected blessing.

Because of a severe draught, Naomi and her husband left Israel to settle in a foreign land—Moab. Her husband died shortly thereafter. Her two sons married women from their Gentile haven. However, before either of the women conceived, both of Naomi's sons died. Naomi was left with two Moabite daughters-in-law—Orpah and Ruth—and without any hope for grandchildren.

It seemed as if Naomi's life was over. She had lost everything. And if that were not enough, it also seemed as if the hand of the Lord had gone against her (Ruth 1:13). She therefore ordered her daughters-in-law to return to their families. Perhaps that way they would have better prospects of making new lives for themselves.

Meanwhile, Naomi had heard that the draught in Israel had lifted. She was determined to go back to her homeland. Orpah decided to return to her own people. However, Ruth refused. When Naomi insisted, Ruth pleaded her case with these memorable words:

- "Don't urge me to leave you or to turn back from you. Where you go I will go, and where you stay I will stay. Your people will be my people and your God my God. Where you die I will die, and there I will be buried. May the Lord deal with me, be it ever so severely, if even death separates you and me." (Ruth 1:16-17)

Despite the resolute faithfulness of her daughter-in-law, Naomi despaired of her faith in the wake of all her misfortune. Upon her return to Bethlehem, she was greeted with excitement by her old friends, but she responded with gloom:

- "Don't call me Naomi [Hebrew for 'pleasant']," she told them. "Call me Mara [Hebrew for 'bitter'], because the Almighty has made my life very bitter. I went away full, but the Lord has brought me back empty. Why call me Naomi? The Lord has afflicted me; the Almighty has brought misfortune upon me." (Ruth 1:20-21)

There are some sorrows that even the faithful cannot endure. There are times when the vicissitudes of life can crush and squeeze us of any remnant of faith; that is, apart from the faithfulness of our Lord.

Back in Israel, Ruth proved her virtue. Instead of receiving the attentions of young suitors, she offered herself to Naomi's near-relative, Boaz. He was one of the men by whom Ruth could legally bear grandchildren for Naomi!

- She [Naomi] added, "That man [Boaz] is our close relative; he is one of our guardian-redeemers." (Ruth 3:20b)

By the inscrutable grace of God working in their lives, Boaz and Ruth were married. Ruth conceived and bore a child named Obed. This turned out to be such a wonderful and unexpected blessing that…

- The women said to Naomi: "Praise be to the Lord, who this day has not left you without a guardian-redeemer. May he become famous throughout Israel! He will renew your life and sustain you in your old age. For your daughter-in-law, who loves you and who is better to you than seven sons, has given him birth." (Ruth 4:14-15)

Back in that day, grandchildren were considered a great blessing, far more than they are today. There is little doubt that the women who spoke these words to Naomi had no idea that their invocation regarding a "guardian-redeemer" would be prophetic. Yet, if we take a close look at the family tree of Naomi, we see just how prescient Naomi's friends were. Her grandson Obed would become the father of Jesse, and Jesse would become the father of David, who would become the King of Israel. And finally, through David would come the ultimate "Guardian-Redeemer," Jesus Christ!

We cannot bear such honor unless we have been prepared for it through periods of tears and loss. The more the well is carved and scraped out, the more water it will hold. The more disappointments and hardships we endure, the greater our capacity to contain blessing. If this were not so, then the weeds of pride and arrogance, which abound in fertile soil, would choke out whatever good might be growing alongside.

We require regular pruning to keep us healthy. Here is what Jesus had to say about this:

- "I am the true vine, and my Father is the gardener. He cuts off every branch in me that bears no fruit, while every branch that does bear fruit he prunes so that it will be even more fruitful." (John 15:1-2)

If not properly pruned, there are some trees that choke and kill themselves because of their own growth. So, the Father prunes the branches of those who are His own. However, we must remember that the Lord is close to those He has cut back, those who are broken-hearted and contrite:

- For this is what the high and lofty One says—
  he who lives forever, whose name is holy:
  "I live in a high and holy place,
  but also with him who is contrite and lowly in spirit,
  to revive the spirit of the lowly
  and to revive the heart of the contrite."
  Isaiah 57:15

- "This is the one I esteem:
  he who is humble and contrite in spirit,
  and trembles at my word."
  Isaiah 66:2b

If we study the lineage of the Messiah in Matthew 1, we will find many who were broken-hearted, many who were humble and contrite. In addition to the foreigner, Ruth, the names of Rahab and Tamar are also mentioned. Rahab was a prostitute who gave shelter to the Israelite spies. She and her family were spared when Jericho was destroyed. Tamar was a woman who had lost a number of husbands. Overlooked and mistreated, she had to seduce her father-in-law, Judah, in order to have children.

It is notable that the ancestry of Jesus presented in Matthew contains only three women, and each of them was a "disgrace" in some way. These were women who, under normal circumstances, could never have hoped to receive such an honor. These peculiar additions to the lineage of Christ preach a message we must not overlook. God has hidden His grace in the midst of the ragged vestures of the broken, in the desperation of the hopeless. Therefore, all who follow Christ— no matter their circumstances—have reason to be of good cheer!

Naomi had no conception of the glory that would proceed from her. She was convinced that she was merely God's throw-away but, all along, He had been preparing for something glorious through her—the advent of the Savior of the world.

Chapter 8

UNDERSTANDING THE BOOK OF JOB

CHAPTER SUMMARY
Job presents us with many mysteries about the purpose of suffering. How do we understand Job's words, the words of His three friends, Elihu, and ultimately, God's words and purposes?

The Book of Job is essentially about our ignorant, self-righteous judgments. One prime example of this is the way that Job's wife had counseled her husband—in the midst of his life-shattering losses—to curse God and die. Before we rehearse the shortcomings of Job's acquaintances—Eliphaz, Bildad and Zophar—we must acknowledge that they were good friends. They sat with Job for a week, mourning with their friend without saying a word. However, in ignorance, they had judged him guilty of committing terrible sins. They were convinced—wrongly—that Job's great and secret sins had brought about the monumental misfortunes that had befallen him.

These friends understood far less than they thought they did. Their understanding of God was severely limited, and their understanding of Job was both degrading and totally off-base. According to Job 1:1 and 1:8, it was Job who had been the most righteous of men. And yet he too had judged God wrongly:

- "Although I am blameless, I have no concern for myself; I despise my own life. It is all the same; that is why I say, 'He destroys both the blameless and the wicked.' When a scourge brings sudden death, he mocks the despair of the innocent. When a land falls into the hands of the wicked, he blindfolds its judges. If it is not he, then who is it?" (Job 9:21-24)

- "I will say to God, 'Do not condemn me; let me know why you contend against me. Does it seem good to you to oppress, to despise the work of your hands and favor the designs of the wicked?'" (Job 10:2-3)

- "All was well with me, but he shattered me; he seized me by the neck and crushed me. He has made me his target; his archers surround me. Without pity, he pierces my kidneys and spills my gall on the ground. Again and again he bursts upon me; he rushes at me like a warrior...yet my hands have been free of violence and my prayer is pure." (Job 16:12-14, 17)

- "As surely as God lives, who has denied me justice, the Almighty, who has made me taste bitterness of soul...my lips will not speak wickedness, and my tongue will utter no deceit." (Job 27:2, 4)

Was Job revealing an accurate assessment of his own character in these verses? Not according to other passages in the narrative:

- These three men ceased to answer Job, because he was righteous in his own eyes. Then Elihu the son of Barachel the Buzite, of the family of Ram, burned with anger. He burned with anger at Job because he justified himself rather than God. (Job 32:1-2)

Elihu did not mince his words when he spoke to Job:

- "But you have said in my hearing—I heard the very words—'I am pure and without sin; I am clean and free from guilt. Yet God has found fault with me; he considers me his enemy. He fastens my feet in shackles; he keeps close watch on all my paths.' But I tell you, in this you are not right, for God is greater than man." (Job 33:8-12)

Is human suffering so difficult for us to understand as to be incomprehensible? Why did Job suffer at God's hand?

One of Job's "complaints" against God was that He would not appear before Job to explain His charges against him. But Elihu's perspective was very different:

- "Why do you contend against him, saying, 'He will answer none of man's words'? For God speaks in one way, and in two, though man does not perceive it. In a dream, in a vision of the night, when deep sleep falls on men, while they slumber on their beds, then he opens the ears of men and terrifies them with warnings, that he may turn man aside from his deed and conceal pride from a man; he keeps back his soul from the pit, his life from perishing by the sword. Man is also rebuked with pain on his bed and with continual strife in his bones, so that his life loathes bread, and his appetite the choicest food. His flesh is so wasted away that it cannot be seen, and his bones that were not seen stick out. His soul draws near the pit, and his life to those who bring death." (Job 33:13-22)

So Elihu, sounding like a prophet, points out persuasively that God indeed had been speaking to Job. However, Job had been too proud to hear Him. When we become convinced of our own righteousness, we harden our hearts and no longer have ears to hear. Even this most righteous of men had become hardened. A hefty dose of affliction would be required to open his ears.

❖ ❖ ❖

According to Elihu, Job needed what all of us sinners need:

- "If there be for him an angel, a mediator, one of the thousand, to declare to man what is right for him, and he is merciful to him, and says, 'Deliver him from going down into the pit; I have found a ransom; let his flesh become fresh with youth; let him return to the days of his youthful vigor'; then man prays to God, and he accepts him; he sees his face with a shout of joy, and he restores to man his righteousness." (Job 33:23-26)

Why would Job require a ransom? After all, we have evidence in Job 1:5 that he had been offering animal sacrifices on a regular basis. Evidently, Elihu was referring to a different kind of ransom, one which required an "angel" or "mediator." Furthermore, there is no indication of any payment of what we might call a "super-ransom." It is as if our Lord is tantalizing us with yet another foreshadowing of Messiah. According to Hebrews 9:14-15, Christ would be the One who would retroactively pay for Job's sins. With very lyrical, beautiful turns of phrases, Elihu paints a picture of what this payment for sin would accomplish:

- "He sings before men and says: 'I sinned and perverted what was right, and it was not repaid to me. He has redeemed my soul from going down into the pit, and my life shall look upon the light.' Behold, God does all these things, twice, three times, with a man, to bring back his soul from the pit, that he may be lighted with the light of life." (Job 33:27-30)

From the perspective of everything that God has done through Christ to save all those who believe in Him from the pit—Hell—we can see clearly the Angel or Mediator that Elihu had in mind!

❖ ❖ ❖

At this point, it does not appear as if Job is really "getting" Elihu's message. Elihu was trying to prepare Job, to persuade him to moderate his position before God's terrifying arrival in a whirlwind. Continuing in this work of preparation, Elihu declared to Job that humankind does not have the wisdom to bring indictments against God:

- "Tell us what we should say to him; we cannot draw up our case because of our darkness. Should he [God] be told that I want to speak? Would any man ask to be swallowed up? Now no one can look at the sun, bright as it is in the skies after the wind has swept them clean. Out of the north he comes in golden splendor; God comes in awesome majesty. The Almighty is beyond our reach and exalted in power…" (Job 37:19-23a)

If we are unable to look at the sun, how could anyone possibly expect to stand before God in an accusing manner? Only someone with a thoroughly inflated estimation of his understanding would be foolhardy enough to attempt such a thing.

In a terrifying manifestation, God confirmed Elihu's denunciation of Job:

- Then the LORD answered Job out of the whirlwind and said: "Who is this that darkens counsel by words without knowledge?" (Job 38:1-2)

In order to make His point clear, God asked Job a series of questions—questions which Job could not even begin to answer. The lesson was plain to see: Job was woefully lacking in the understanding necessary to bring any indictment against God. In fact, no one can do this. Here is the way that God addressed this truth with Job:

- "Would you discredit my justice? Would you condemn me to justify yourself?" (Job 40:8)

This is exactly what Job had been doing. And this is exactly what we do when we experience trials. Because we are so ignorant in our understanding, we blame God for any alleged wrong or difficulty that we are going through.

Job had been prideful and self-righteous. In love, God had corrected him so that he would not perish and be condemned to "the pit." However, Job chose rather to blame God and assert his own righteousness. Therefore God, because of His love for Job, used mighty afflictions to bring him to repentance.

Perhaps the higher our spiritual kite flies, the more we need God to bring us down so that we can clearly see our true status. Finally, Job saw things as they really were. In fact, he repented mightily:

- "I am unworthy [vile, NKJV]—how can I reply to you? I put my hand over my mouth. I spoke once, but I have no answer—twice, but I will say no more." (Job 40:4-5)

- "You asked, 'Who is this that obscures my counsel without knowledge?' Surely I spoke of things I did not understand, things too wonderful for me to know...My ears had heard of you but now my eyes have seen you. Therefore I despise myself and repent in dust and ashes." (Job 42:3, 5-6)

Job was finally able to see what God was doing in his life through all his afflictions.

Meanwhile, according to *The Jewish Study Bible,* Job had nothing to repent of or confess! Therefore, his "Suffering is incomprehensible." The commentators of that Bible are culpable of understanding and judging God wrongly. They are guilty of leaning much too heavily on their own limited understanding of God and His ways. This is exactly what Job had done before he repented. Conversely, this is what the Word says we are to do:

- Trust in the LORD with all your heart and lean not on your own understanding; in all your ways acknowledge him, and he will make your paths straight. (Proverbs 3:5-6)

❖ ❖ ❖

Finally, let us take a look at the way that God corrected Job's three friends:

- After the Lord had said these things to Job, he said to Eliphaz the Temanite, "I am angry with you and your two friends, because you have not spoken of me what is right, as my servant Job has. So now take seven bulls and seven rams and go to my servant Job and sacrifice a burnt offering for yourselves. My servant Job will pray for you, and I will accept his prayer and not deal with you according to your folly. You have not spoken of me what is right, as my servant Job has." (Job 42:7-8)

The friends of Job had misjudged both God and Job and needed correction. However, doesn't it seem as if God is contradicting Himself? Two times He makes the charge that Job's friends "have not spoken of me what is right, *as my servant Job has.*" However, before Job had repented, God had clearly accused him of not speaking rightly about Him.

Is this in fact a contradiction? Not really. Why not? Simply because, when we confess our sins, according to 1 John 1:9, He forgives us and cleanses us. Job had learned his lesson, and God had wiped his slate clean.

- Mercy triumphs over judgment! (James 2:13b)

God wants to give us the world. He even gave Job twice as much as he had before. However, the more He fills our cup, the more He must first *empty* it and *cleanse* it from any contaminants. That way, it is safe for Him to fill it again…to overflowing!

Chapter 9

UNDERSTANDING THE GIFT OF THE PSALMS

CHAPTER SUMMARY

The Psalms enable us to bridge the chasm between our present disappointing circumstances and the promises of God. The Psalms provide us with a valuable record of how the psalmists were able to advance from pain to praise.

I have been so distressed to hear about the ever-increasing number of young people who have left the Church and its faith. From what I can gather, their expectations about God and His promises are not in line with the reality of what they are actually experiencing in their lives.

Here is a short list of some of their "lamentations":

I prayed and trusted, but God didn't answer my prayers.

I asked for His guidance, but He has remained silent.

I was confident that He had led me to marry, but now I am not so sure. My wife left me for another guy, and I no longer trust Him.

My own story had very similar overtones. I was trying to follow Christ the best I could, but it wasn't good enough. I became overwhelmed with depression and panic attacks. Some days I was so distressed that I couldn't even get out of bed. It seemed to me that God was refusing to answer my prayers. I couldn't understand why He was allowing me to suffer so much. He promised me His comfort, and I could see that blessing in the lives of others, but not for me. He promised to love me, but I felt totally unloved, unlovable, and utterly rejected. He promised that He would never leave me, but I felt entirely abandoned. From my perspective, the Christian life was turning out to be a huge fraud.

If I would have had a viable alternative, I would have gladly "jumped ship." I was clearly at a dead end. I had already tried every promising option, and each one had failed me. Either God would somehow come through…or I was finished.

God's silence convinced me of either one of two things: Either I was so worthless that God wouldn't waste His time on me—or God did not exist. And if that was the case, then everything I had experienced of God was merely self-deception.

Since I had nowhere else to turn, I began to read the Psalms. I found that the psalmists had some of the same kinds of problems that I did. This provided me some measure of comfort, but I was quickly confronted with a powerful doubt. Were the Psalms truly inspired and "God-breathed," as 2 Timothy 3:16 clearly declares? So many of the Psalms portrayed overflowing expressions of human feelings. How could they possibly be the Word of God?

After further study, I was greatly encouraged. It was plain to see that Jesus regarded the Psalms on a totally equal footing with the rest of the Scriptures. For example, let's take a look at what happened after His resurrection, when He appeared to His disciples who had been hiding behind closed doors:

- Then he said to them, "These are my words that I spoke to you while I was still with you, that everything written about me in the Law of Moses and the Prophets and the Psalms must be fulfilled." Then he opened their minds to understand the Scriptures. (Luke 24:44-45)

In Jesus' mind, the Psalms stood tall, fully inspired and fully to be trusted, right along-side "the Law of Moses and the Prophets." Furthermore, the way that Jesus had repeatedly quoted from the Psalms proved as well that He regarded them as Scripture:

- Jesus said to them, "Have you never read in the Scriptures: 'The stone that the builders rejected has become the cornerstone; this was the Lord's doing, and it is marvelous in our eyes'?" (Matthew 21:42, quoting Psalm 118)

After this, Jesus asked the Pharisees a rhetorical question about a Psalm that they regarded as Messianic. He was trying to demonstrate for them the pre-existence of the Messiah:

- "What do you think about the Christ? Whose son is he?" They said to him, "The son of David." He said to them, "How is it then that David, in the Spirit, calls him Lord, saying, 'The Lord said to my Lord, "Sit at my right hand, until I put your enemies under your feet'?" (Matthew 22:42-44, quoting Psalm 110)

Of course Jesus would use one of the Psalms to make His point. And why not? The Psalms are an essential component among many in the Hebrew canon of inspired writings. Our Lord knew it…and so did the Pharisees.

Based on the Gospels as well as the epistles, the consistent testimony of the New Testament is that the Apostles regarded the Psalms—perhaps the most quoted book in the Bible—as inspired.

I began to understand that our Lord was fully able to weave the psalmists' very human outpourings of grief and emotion into a wholly divine fabric. I studied the Psalms in earnest, ready and willing to receive the divine wisdom and guidance I needed so that I could live my life.

Here is one of the gems I discovered. I noticed that David had complained:

- How long, O LORD? Will you forget me forever? How long will you hide your face from me? How long must I take counsel in my soul and have sorrow in my heart all the day? How long shall my enemy be exalted over me? (Psalm 13:1-2)

This Psalm made me think. David had been the man "after God's own heart," and yet he had suffered so much torment. God had promised David that He would never leave him, that He would establish an everlasting kingdom through one of his descendants. How then could David feel so forsaken? It is clear that he had been praying to God, but God did not seem to be answering him. And yet, we know that God had not rejected David.

Perhaps He had not rejected me.

❖ ❖ ❖

Many of the psalmists brought their complaints before the Lord concerning His chosen people, the Israelites. In light of the glowing expectations of peace and well-being based on God's promises, the difficulties that the Hebrews suffered again and again did not seem to match the blessings that were promised.

First, let us look at the psalmist Ethan's "review" of God's glorious promises to King David:

- "I [God] will maintain my love to him [David] forever, and my covenant with him will never fail...I will not violate my covenant or alter what my lips have uttered. Once for all, I have sworn by my holiness—and I will not lie to David—that his line will continue forever and his throne endure before me like the sun; it will be established forever like the moon, the faithful witness in the sky." (Psalm 89:28, 34-37)

However, by the next verse, Ethan's tone had changed dramatically. He even began to accuse God of unfaithfulness:

- But you have rejected, you have spurned, you have been very angry with your anointed one. You have renounced the covenant with your servant and have defiled his crown in the dust. You have broken through all his walls and reduced his strongholds to ruins…O Lord, where is your former great love, which in your faithfulness you swore to David? (Psalm 89:38-40, 49)

According to Ethan, God had betrayed His people and had reneged on His promises. Israel's degraded status had failed to measure up to what God had promised them. Ethan seemed to be rejecting the faith of his Fathers.

I was Inexorably drawn into this perplexing drama, and I wasn't alone in my sense of betrayal. Besides Ethan, other psalmists had also felt betrayed by God; they felt as if He had failed to live up to His promises. For example, the psalmist Asaph believed that he been let down by God. From what he could see, it seemed to him as if the arrogant enemies of God were living in far better circumstances than the righteous. Therefore, he poured out his complaint:

- Surely in vain have I kept my heart pure; in vain have I washed my hands in innocence. (Psalm 73:13)

According to Asaph, serving God had turned out to be disappointing.

These psalmists had been exemplars of the faith, and yet they were coming to the conclusion that their faith had been a waste of time. The testimonies of these and other psalmists sound just like what young people today are saying—young people who are departing from the faith.

Even the Messiah claimed that His Father had abandoned Him:

- My God, my God, why have you forsaken me? Why are you so far from saving me, so far from the words of my groaning? (Psalm 22:1)

However, we know from the advantage of hindsight that this abandonment had only been temporary. By the end of the Psalm, Jesus proclaimed that His experience of being forsaken would not be the end of the story:

- For he has not despised or disdained the suffering of the afflicted one; he has not hidden his face from him but has listened to his cry for help. (Psalm 22:24)

Was there a lesson here for me? Maybe I also had failed to see the big picture. I wondered if I was suffering from a monumental case of myopia.

But what about the psalmist Ethan? Did he resolve His conflict with God? Here is how he concluded Psalm 89:

- Praise be to the LORD forever! Amen and Amen. (Psalm 89:52)

From the verses in Psalm 89 that were mentioned earlier, it does not seem as if Ethan was able to see the big picture—that God would once again exalt His nation and show Himself faithful to His Covenant and His promises to David. However, it does seem—evident in the words of his conclusion in v. 52—

that Ethan at least had come to the realization that there was much more to the picture than what he was able to see.

Perhaps there was more to my suffering than what I was able to see. Perhaps my Savior had secretly been loving me in the midst of my tears. Perhaps my Savior had been suffering right along with me:

- For we do not have a high priest who is unable to sympathize with our weaknesses, but we have one who has been tempted in every way, just as we are—yet without sin. (Hebrews 4:15)

❖ ❖ ❖

There is a postscript to the story of Asaph, the psalmist who—in Psalm 73—was so disappointed as he served God. It turns out that he was subsequently blessed with a revelation. He entered the Temple and was shown the big picture. He perceived that the prospering of the arrogant and the suffering of the righteous were only temporary. After what had been revealed to him, he made this grateful proclamation:

- I was senseless and ignorant; I was a brute beast before you. Yet I am always with you; you hold me by my right hand. You guide me with your counsel, and afterward you will take me into glory. Whom have I in heaven but you? And earth has nothing I desire besides you. My flesh and my heart may fail, but God is the strength of my heart and my portion forever. (Psalm 73:22-26)

Asaph had not been able to perceive of any possible resolution for the conflict in his soul. The arrogant were indeed prospering and the righteous were suffering. And yet, there came a time when God showed him otherwise. By God's grace, he had been enabled to see beyond his limited experiences and observations.

Could it be that there was something I was missing? Was there indeed a purpose for my suffering, as there had been for Asaph? Maybe I was expecting too much—immediate understanding about what I was suffering. Finally, could it be that those who are leaving the Church are expecting too much? It could be that they are not yet ready to see the big picture of God's plan. Perhaps God's will is for them to walk by faith and not by sight.

Why is it that some people persevere and continue to look towards God—even in the midst of their perplexity—while others leave their faith behind? I cannot answer this question. I only pray that those who leave will return once more to our only possible Hope.

Meanwhile, I sincerely thank God for what I suffered. I liken myself to David, who confessed:

- It was good for me to be afflicted so that I might learn your decrees. The law from your mouth is more precious to me than thousands of pieces of silver and gold. (Psalm 119:71-72)

We all struggle with many disappointments. We sometimes find ourselves baffled that our present situation is at such odds with the divinely promised joy of salvation and victory over sin. The Psalms are able to take us by the hand when we need it, to guide us over what seems to be the impassable chasm between our present disappointments and the promises of God. These inspired songs can open our eyes to the big picture...just as they restored the psalmists Ethan and Asaph to the sincere and full praise of God.

Chapter 10

UNDERSTANDING ECCLESIASTES

CHAPTER SUMMARY

In order to make sense of this book, we must understand it from Solomon's perspective. It represented his quest for the wisdom to discover the meaning of life. However, because of his inadequate understanding of the afterlife, Solomon was unable to discover life's full meaning.

The Book of Ecclesiastes does not surrender its jewels easily. There are formidable challenges for the interpreter. Nevertheless, I believe that when we find its key, we will be able to unlock the door to the copious treasure within. And what's more, the book gives us valuable clues, even from the very beginning, as to the whereabouts of this significant "key."

- The words of the Preacher, the son of David, king in Jerusalem. Vanity of vanities, says the Preacher, vanity of vanities! *All is vanity.* (Ecclesiastes 1:1-2, emphasis added)

"All is vanity." What an amazingly all-inclusive statement! But there's more. According to Solomon, this pervasive vanity includes not just the present, but the future—everything that *will* happen:

- So if a person lives many years, let him rejoice in them all; but let him remember that the days of darkness will be many. *All that comes is vanity.* (Ecclesiastes 11:8, emphasis added)

Not only in this life but in whatever happens after it—according to Solomon's understanding—*all is vanity.*

These opening verses of the book contradict a commonly-held view among believers that everything is vanity... *except for the life devoted to God.* Surprisingly, Solomon claims that even serving God is a "vain" endeavor:

- There is nothing better for a person than that he should eat and drink and find enjoyment in his toil. This also, I saw, is from the hand of God, for apart from him who can eat or who can have enjoyment? For to the one who pleases him God has given wisdom and knowledge and joy, but to the sinner he has given the business of gathering and collecting, only to give to one who pleases God. This also is vanity and a striving after wind. (Ecclesiastes 2:24-26)

Skipping to the end of the book, we discover that Solomon concludes—apart from the final six verses—in the same way that he began:

- Vanity of vanities, says the Preacher; all is vanity. (Ecclesiastes 12:8)

Thus, if we are to take Solomon at his word, the *all* in "all is vanity" would necessarily include serving God. In fact, there is not one verse in the whole book that claims that everything is vanity *except for serving God.*

We know that serving the Lord is clearly not in vain. To help us to wrap our minds around these ideas, I suggest that we understand the word "vanity" as "incomprehensible." With his wisdom, Solomon had been trying to understand the meaning of life. Since this wisdom was unable to penetrate the veil into the next life, Solomon was left frustrated and called it all "incomprehensible."

❖ ❖ ❖

Even after he had attained a great measure of wisdom, Solomon remained unsatisfied by what he found:

- And I applied my heart to seek and to search out by wisdom all that is done under heaven. It is an unhappy business that God has given to the children of man to be busy with. I have seen everything that is done under the sun, and behold, all is vanity [or "incomprehensible"] and a striving after wind. What is crooked cannot be made straight, and what is lacking cannot be counted. I said in my heart, "I have acquired great wisdom, surpassing all who were over Jerusalem before me, and my heart has had great experience of wisdom and knowledge." And I applied my heart to know wisdom and to know madness and folly. I perceived that this also is but a striving after wind. (Ecclesiastes 1:13-17)

Solomon tried to understand life from every angle, even from the perspective of "madness and folly." But nothing was able to give him the understanding he sought. What he found instead was that his search for wisdom was like trying to grasp the wind, an impossible undertaking. Sadly for Solomon, he was unable to grasp the larger purposes or meaning of life:

- For in much wisdom is much vexation, and he who increases knowledge increases sorrow. (Ecclesiastes 1:18)

Why did Solomon's gift of wisdom cause him such sorrow and frustration? He still hadn't found what he was looking for:

- Then I considered all that my hands had done and the toil I had expended in doing it, and behold, all was vanity [or "incomprehensible"] and a striving after wind, and there was nothing to be gained under the sun. (Ecclesiastes 2:11)

Solomon had been a great builder and had accomplished many things. How could he conclude that everything he had done was a "striving after the wind"? Simply this: Without the knowledge and assurance of an afterlife, the life he lived in this world—even as a great and wise king—made little sense to him.

- The wise person has his eyes in his head, but the fool walks in darkness. And yet I perceived that the same event happens to all of them. Then I said in my heart, "What happens to the fool will happen to me also. Why then have I been so very wise?" And I said in my heart that this also is vanity. For of the wise as of the fool there is no enduring remembrance, seeing that in the days to come all will have been long forgotten. How the wise dies just like the fool! So I hated life, because what is done under the sun was grievous to me, for all is vanity [or "incomprehensible"] and a striving after wind. (Ecclesiastes 2:14-17)

From the perspective of his wisdom and what his eyes had seen, it did not ultimately matter whether a person was wise or foolish. Both the wise and the foolish would one day die and be forgotten. From what Solomon knew, there was no certainty of an afterlife. And without this assurance, Solomon hated his life. That is why he came to the conclusion that it is a good idea to enjoy life—this life—here and now:

- I hated all my toil in which I toil under the sun, seeing that I must leave it to the man who will come after me, and who knows whether he will be wise or a fool? Yet he will be master of all for which I toiled and used my wisdom under the sun. This also is vanity. So I turned about and gave my heart up to despair over all the toil of my labors under the sun, because sometimes a person who has toiled with wisdom and knowledge and skill must leave everything to be enjoyed by someone who did not toil for it. This also is vanity and a great evil. What has a man from all the toil and striving of heart with which he toils beneath the sun? For all his days are full of sorrow, and his work is a vexation. Even in the night his heart does not rest. This also is vanity. There is nothing better for a person than that he should eat and drink and find enjoyment in his toil. This also, I saw, is from the hand of God. (Ecclesiastes 2:18-24)

These words raise several questions. Once again, did Solomon have any knowledge at all of the afterlife? It doesn't seem that he did. The Five Books of Moses make no explicit mention of such a concept. The blessings that God had promised to Israel for their obedience never included eternal life. Any promise of an afterlife is conspicuously absent. Thus, it should be no surprise to learn that there is no clear indication of eternal life within the pages of Solomon's quintessential book of wisdom, Proverbs.

And yet, we are well aware that there are references to eternal life in the Psalms of Solomon's father, David:

- Surely goodness and mercy shall follow me all the days of my life, and I shall dwell in the house of the LORD forever. (Psalm 23:6; see also Psalms 16:11; 17:15)

Although we might conclude that Solomon must have at least known about eternal life, it is quite clear that he did not internalize this truth, or take it for his own. Perhaps he did not know whether he should take these assurances literally.

Solomon's perspective is clearly seen in verses like the following:

- For what happens to the children of man and what happens to the beasts is the same; as one dies, so dies the other. They all have the same breath, and man has no advantage over the beasts, for all is vanity. All go to one place. All are from the dust, and to dust all return. Who knows whether the spirit of man goes upward and the spirit of the beast goes down into the earth? So I saw that there is nothing better than that a man should rejoice in his work, for that is his lot. Who can bring him to see what will be after him? (Ecclesiastes 3:19-22)

How is it that we might explain the absence of any mention of the afterlife in the writings of Solomon? Perhaps the answer can be found as we consider the gift that he had received from God—wisdom. For, it was indeed wisdom that was his preoccupation during his years-long search for the ultimate meaning of life. However, as laudable and storied as the wisdom of Solomon came to be, such a single-minded focus seems to have left little room for another essential element in his quest for meaning—prayer. In the whole of the Book of Ecclesiastes, there is not one reference to prayer.

Meanwhile, each of the psalms of David could be considered a prayer to God!

❖ ❖ ❖

Therefore, using only his God-given wisdom, Solomon came to some erroneous conclusions:

- It is the same for all, since the same event happens to the righteous and the wicked, to the good and the evil, to the clean and the unclean, to him who sacrifices and him who does not sacrifice. As the good one is, so is the sinner, and he who swears is as he who shuns an oath. This is an evil in all that is done under the sun, that the same event happens to all. Also, the hearts of the children of man are full of evil, and madness is in their hearts while they live, and after that they go to the dead. But he who is joined with all the living has hope, for a living dog is better than a dead lion. For the living know that they will die, but the dead know nothing, and they have no more reward, for the memory of them is forgotten. Their love and their hate and their envy have already perished, and forever they have no more share in all that is done under the sun. Go, eat your bread with joy, and drink your wine with a merry heart, for God has already approved what you do. Let your garments be always white. Let not oil be lacking on your head. Enjoy life with the wife whom you love, all the days of your vain life that he has given you under the sun, because that is your portion in life and in your toil at which you toil under the sun. Whatever your hand finds to do, do it with your might, for there is no work or thought or knowledge or wisdom in Sheol, to which you are going. (Ecclesiastes 9:2-10)

Having no internalized assurance of an afterlife, Solomon wrongly concluded:

1. The sinner and the righteous await the same fate.

2. Hope is merely a matter of life in the here-and-now.

3. Those who are dead have no consciousness.

4. There is no life or existence in Sheol.

Seeing that Solomon was so utterly mistaken, how is it that Ecclesiastes came to be included in the canon of Hebrew Scripture? Why should we regard this book as the Word of God?

First of all, when understood properly, this book contains vital truths. We need to remember that the Bible often uses the errant words of mortals to shed light on God's higher purposes. In fact, there are many words included in the Scriptures that present ideas that are totally in error. To cite just one example from the Book of Job, we learn that God was very angry with the friends of Job:

- After the LORD had said these things to Job, he said to Eliphaz the Temanite, "I am angry with you and your two friends, because you have not spoken of me what is right, as your servant Job has." (Job 42:8)

Even though the words of Jobs' friends were often off-the-mark, God used what those men said to play a part in the accomplishing of His purposes. Thus, even the words of errant men are part of the fabric of inerrant Scripture.

This same principle seems to pertain to Ecclesiastes. Without the full revelation of an afterlife—which God had gradually made known to Israel—Solomon was tormented and even hated life.

We who live in the glorious light of New Testament revelation might be inclined to take the idea of the afterlife for granted. However, we see from the writings of Solomon what can happen to even the greatest of men who do not stand firmly on this foundational knowledge:

- In the day of prosperity be joyful, and in the day of adversity consider: God has made the one as well as the other, so that man may not find out anything that will be after him. In my vain life I have seen everything. There is a righteous man who perishes in his righteousness, and there is a wicked man who prolongs his life in his evildoing. Be not overly righteous, and do not make yourself too wise. Why should you destroy yourself? Be not overly wicked, neither be a fool. Why should you die before your time? (Ecclesiastes 7:14-17)

We are perplexed by Solomon's conclusion that we are to live as if this is our only life. It is shocking to read, "Be not overly righteous, and do not make yourself too wise." These ideas fly in the face of the truth we find in the rest of the Bible. However, from the perspective of Solomon's quest for wisdom—and knowing that he lacked the assurance of eternal life—his conclusions make perfect sense. In fact, Solomon's words can provide us with valuable insight into the secular mind-set of our day. We can more easily understand the bleak future that awaits those without God. For them, life is like what Solomon had written:

- So if a person lives many years, let him rejoice in them all; but let him remember that the days of darkness will be many. All that comes is vanity [or, "incomprehensible"]. (Ecclesiastes 11:8)

When we who believe see the words, "…but let him remember that the days of darkness will be many," perhaps our sense of empathy for those who are lost will be rekindled.

Let us keep in mind that Solomon was at least hoping to understand the meaning of life. Those who do not know God and are secular in their thinking are in another category altogether. They do not believe that there is any meaning in life. To them, our very existence is just an accident. Therefore, they must carve out their own little sanctuary of meaning and fulfillment in whatever ways they can. In contrast, Solomon was at least willing to accept from God's hand any limited morsels of understanding that He might choose to offer.

❖ ❖ ❖

As burdensome as the quest for wisdom had become for Solomon, he still affirmed it in a limited way, as it pertains to this world:

- Then I saw that there is more gain in wisdom than in folly, as there is more gain in light than in darkness. The wise person has his eyes in his head, but the fool walks in darkness. And yet I perceived that the same event happens to all of them. (Ecclesiastes 2:13-14)

- Wisdom is good with an inheritance, an advantage to those who see the sun. For the protection of wisdom is like the protection of money, and the advantage of knowledge is that wisdom preserves the life of him who has it. (Ecclesiastes 7:11-12)

- Wisdom gives strength to the wise man more than ten rulers who are in a city. (Ecclesiastes 7:19)

- If the iron is blunt, and one does not sharpen the edge, he must use more strength, but wisdom helps one to succeed. (Ecclesiastes 10:10)

Nevertheless, Solomon's affirmation of temporal wisdom is counter-balanced by his disappointment with the limits of that wisdom:

- All this I have tested by wisdom. I said, "I will be wise," but it was far from me. That which has been is far off, and deep, very deep; who can find it out? (Ecclesiastes 7:23-24)

Even Solomon's surpassing wisdom was not able to reach beyond the veil and into the next life. And without that essential illumination, the apex of wisdom that Solomon was seeking eluded him:

- When I applied my heart to know wisdom, and to see the business that is done on earth, how neither day nor night do one's eyes see sleep, then I saw all the work of God, that man cannot find out the work that is done under the sun. However much man may toil in seeking, he will not find it out. Even though a wise man claims to know, he cannot find it out. (Ecclesiastes 8:16-17)

Solomon's understanding was unable to penetrate into God's secrets. There are truths that are available to us, but only through God's willingness to share them. In fact, the Apostle Paul also affirmed the apparent meaninglessness of life when it is devoid of further disclosures from God:

- If in Christ we have hope in this life only, we are of all people most to be pitied...What do I gain if, humanly speaking, I fought with beasts at Ephesus? If the dead are not raised, "Let us eat and drink, for tomorrow we die." (1 Corinthians 15:19, 32)

If no eternal inheritance awaits us in heaven, then our lives on earth would truly be meaningless—here today and gone tomorrow. Like beasts, we would be condemned to an existence of fighting to stay alive to enjoy the little that we might have in the moment.

However, that is not the inheritance of the believer in Christ. Our Lord has opened the way for us to come to Him. He has opened our minds through His Word so that we can see the big picture—the grand picture—our hope of eternal joy! Because of this greater light that we now have, Paul was able to say:

- For I consider that the sufferings of this present time are not worth comparing with the glory that is to be revealed to us. (Romans 8:18)

How could the Old Testament Jewish believer endure suffering without the clear revelation of an eternity of joy? I don't see how. Instead, by God's grace, we have been empowered and enabled to endure suffering in the same way that Jesus endured it—by looking ahead to the joy:

- Therefore, since we are surrounded by so great a cloud of witnesses, let us also lay aside every weight, and sin which clings so closely, and let us run with endurance the race that is set before us, looking to Jesus, the founder and perfecter of our faith, who for the joy that was set before him endured the cross, despising the shame, and is seated at the right hand of the throne of God. (Hebrews 12:1-2)

We can endure the temporary suffering of this life because we can look ahead to an eternity of joy. This is similar to the way we are able to endure being sick when we know that it will last for only a few days.

Finally, we cannot rejoice in our suffering in this world as we should, unless we understand that it has a blessed purpose. Here is what Scripture says:

- In this you rejoice, though now for a little while, if necessary, you have been grieved by various trials...Though you have not seen him, you love him. Though you do not now see him, you believe in him and rejoice with joy that is inexpressible and filled with glory, obtaining the outcome of your faith, the salvation of your souls. (1 Peter 1:6, 8-9)

❖ ❖ ❖

Even atheists realize that gratitude is essential to a life that is well-lived. However, it is difficult to be grateful for a life that promises only suffering, decline, and the finality of death.

Instead, we have been granted the priceless knowledge of our ultimate, benign future and the hope that comes with it. Solomon had no such hope. That is why he found life burdensome and its pain unbearable.

I wonder whether we adequately understand the tremendous gift of the hope we have in Christ. To cite just one example of the many hope-building blessings that we have been given, Jesus counseled that there is no need for us to worry about those who might take our lives:

- "And do not fear those who kill the body but cannot kill the soul. Rather fear him [God] who can destroy both soul and body in hell." (Matthew 10:28)

We need not worry about our temporal welfare. The span of our lives is just a flicker in time. Oh yes, we still worry. But think about what it would be like if we did not have the hope of eternal life with our Savior!

We are also free from any compulsion to take revenge:

- Do you not know that you are God's temple and that God's Spirit dwells in you? If anyone destroys God's temple, God will destroy him. For God's temple is holy, and you are that temple. (1 Corinthians 3:16-17)

Instead of seeking revenge, we are free to love our enemies and not hate them, for we know that God's justice will ultimately triumph:

- Only let your manner of life be worthy of the gospel of Christ, so that whether I come and see you or am absent, I may hear of you that you are standing firm in one spirit, with one mind striving side by side for the faith of the gospel, and not frightened in anything by your opponents. This is a clear sign to them of their destruction, but of your salvation, and that from God. (Philippians 1:27-28)

It is the hope of eternal life that enables us to look into the face of our suffering with a smile. Without such a hope, we would be like Solomon. Even though he had everything that this world has to offer—wives, wealth, honor, adulation, and more wisdom than any other man—he was miserable:

- I hated all my toil in which I toil under the sun, seeing that I must leave it to the man who will come after me, and who knows whether he will be wise or a fool? Yet he will be master of all for which I toiled and used my wisdom under the sun. This also is vanity. So I turned about and gave my heart up to despair over all the toil of my labors under the sun. (Ecclesiastes 2:18-20)

We have something far more valuable than what Solomon had in all his glory. We have the confidence that comes from the knowledge that we will be with our Lord for all eternity!

Chapter 11

UNDERSTANDING THE PROPHETS OF ISRAEL

CHAPTER SUMMARY

The Hebrew prophets were not mindless instruments of God. Just like us, they too struggled with the Word of God. God wanted His prophets to understand Him properly so that they would become fit representatives. Therefore, He subjected them to numerous learning experiences.

For a long time, I tended to see the prophets as little more than robots. God told them to speak, and they spoke. The Lord gave them instructions, and they followed them.

However, I began to see that the prophets, in many ways, were very much like us. They even had issues with the words of God. Simply put, they did not always see things as God saw them. In particular, they had considerable difficulty understanding God's righteous judgments, especially those judgments that He pronounced against His own people, the Jews.

Jeremiah was convinced that God's damning assessment of Israel was way off. He thought it would be easy to find at least one person who was walking with the Lord, especially if he looked among the educated:

- I thought, "These are only the poor; they are foolish, for they do not know the way of the LORD, the requirements of their God. So I will go to the leaders and speak to them; surely they know the way of the LORD, the requirements of their God." (Jeremiah 5:4-5)

Jeremiah was like the rest of us. He thought that God's appraisals were overly harsh and that His threats of judgment were inappropriate. He was convinced that the educated elite were of a wholly superior caliber. Surely they would merit forgiveness and not judgment.

Are we not just like Jeremiah? Are we not guilty of seeing as he did, with rose-colored glasses? After all, we—like Jeremiah—find little in our peers and colleagues or family that merits divine judgment. Our friends kiss their wives goodbye in the morning and tell stories to their children at night. They are respected at their jobs and get promotions. They are honored by the communities in which they live. They might not be perfect, but then again—who is? Surely they are not in the same category of sinners as drunkards or wife-beaters. Clearly, those are the kinds of people who deserve judgment.

According to Scripture, fine appearances can, at times, be deceiving. In the Book of Romans, Paul quoted and affirmed the Old Testament's assessment of human degradation:

- As it is written: "There is no one righteous, not even one; there is no one who understands, no one who seeks God. All have turned away, they have together become worthless; there is no one who does good, not even one." (Romans 3:10-12)

If we fail to understand this cardinal truth, then we will erroneously remain convinced that humanity requires only a face-lift, and not a complete overhaul. Likewise, if we fail to understand the necessity for God's judgment, we will also fail to grasp God's radically undeserved grace.

These hard truths must become foundational in our lives if we are to serve God and represent Him faithfully. When we fail to realize that everything we receive from God is because of His mercy and not because of our merit, we become intolerably arrogant. It is for this very reason that our Savior chooses the foolish and the weak and the low—those who realize that they deserve the least (1 Corinthians 1:26-29)—to serve Him. In His wisdom, He ordained that salvation should be entirely a matter of God's free gift to us, which precludes any and all boasting on our part:

- For by grace you have been saved through faith. And this is not your own doing; it is the gift of God, not a result of works, so that no one may boast. (Ephesians 2:8-9; see also Romans 3:21-28).

In contrast to the way God sees things, we tend to regard some people as more worthy candidates for salvation than others. In this way, we honor some and dishonor the rest. However, Jesus adamantly denied that any of us are worthy of the kingdom of heaven (Matthew 19:23-26; Luke 18:9-14). Salvation is all about God's merit and has nothing to do with our own (Titus 3:3-7). If we fail to understand this, we cannot give God the worship He requires and deserves. Jesus taught that we are to worship God in spirit—in the depths of our being—and in truth (John 4:22-24). This means that He is to receive all the praise and glory.

This understanding of God and the way He works is essential if we are to flourish in our relationships within the context of the Church. When the church at Corinth strayed from an honest assessment of their humble estate, love was soon replaced by conflict, and unity by factionalism. Some in the church there began to boast about the way they had aligned themselves with the very best preachers and teachers. Paul warned them that this kind of bragging was highly destructive of Christian fellowship:

- Now, brothers and sisters, I have applied these things to myself and Apollos for your benefit, so that you may learn from us the meaning of the saying, "Do not go beyond what is written." Then you will not be puffed up in being a follower of one of us over against the other. For who makes you different from anyone else? What do you have that you did not receive? And if you did receive it, why do you boast as though you did not? (I Corinthians 4:6-7)

Such boasting not only undermines human relationships, it also jeopardizes our relationship with God.

❖ ❖ ❖

If Jeremiah was going to serve God faithfully, he would also need to learn to see as God sees. And there would be no better place to learn this skill than in his hometown of Anathoth. Jeremiah had come from a respectable family, a family of priests. However, he soon learned that there were those in this town who wanted to kill him because of the Word of God:

- Then the LORD told me about the plots my enemies were making against me. I had been as unaware as a lamb on the way to its slaughter. I had no idea that they were planning to kill me! (Jeremiah 11:18-19)

And this was only the beginning. The Lord then warned Jeremiah:

- "Even your own brothers, members of your own family, have turned on you. They have plotted, raising a cry against you. Do not trust them, no matter how pleasantly they speak." (Jeremiah 12:6).

Jeremiah was beginning to see what it meant to truly follow and identify with the Lord. Not only had Israel turned against their God, they had also turned against the bearer of His Word, Jeremiah:

- Then I said, "What sadness is mine, my mother. Oh, that I had died at birth! I am hated everywhere I go. I am neither a lender who has threatened to foreclose nor a borrower who refuses to pay—yet they all curse me." (Jeremiah 15:10)

It is inevitable that when we experience rejection first-hand, there is a direct impact on the way we regard the rest of humanity. And so it was with Jeremiah. Before his rejection at the hands of his own townsmen, he had struggled with what he thought was God's lack of compassion for Israel:

- O Hope of Israel, its Savior in times of distress, why are you like a stranger in the land, like a traveler who stays only a night? Why are you like a man taken by surprise, like a warrior powerless to save? You are among us, O LORD, and we bear your name; do not forsake us! (Jeremiah 14:8-9)

However, after Jeremiah experienced the same kind of rejection that God routinely experiences, his pleas for compassion fall silent. In fact, he begins to ask for the very thing that he had been so vehemently against—judgment!

- Then I said, "LORD, you know I am suffering for your sake. Punish my persecutors! Don't let them kill me! Be merciful to me and give them what they deserve!" (Jeremiah 15:15)

Experience can be a great teacher. Here is another quote that showcases Jeremiah's new attitude:

- "LORD, you know all about their murderous plots against me. Don't forgive their crimes and blot out their sins. Let them die before you. Deal with them in your anger." (Jeremiah 18:23)

After we have walked a few steps in our Lord's despised shoes, the idea of judgment becomes far more acceptable.

❖ ❖ ❖

Before we can truly understand the mercy of God, we first have to understand the righteousness of God. Jeremiah was learning about justice and righteousness and had swung far to the side of judgment without mercy. Soon, he would be ready to learn about mercy, but not just yet. At this point, he was still longing to see God's vengeance:

- "LORD Almighty! You know those who are righteous, and you examine the deepest thoughts of hearts and minds. Let me see your vengeance against them, for I have committed my cause to you." (Jeremiah 20:12)

Once again, we understand God through the lens of our experience. When we find acceptance from those around us, we ask God for His compassion on them. When we see the world from this perspective, we appreciate God's reticence to execute judgment. Conversely, when we don't experience acceptance, neither do we want our detractors to experience God's mercy. Instead, we ask God for judgment and are disturbed when the judgment is slow in coming. Jeremiah had yet to learn about God's mercy for the undeserving.

Israel had rejected God. In fact, Israel had rejected God more completely than any other nation had rejected their evil and worthless gods:

- "Go west to the land of Cyprus; go east to the land of Kedar. Think about what you see there. See if anyone has ever heard of anything as strange as this. Has any nation ever exchanged its gods for another god, even though its gods are nothing? Yet my people have exchanged their glorious God for worthless idols!" (Jeremiah 2:10-11)

It is only after we understand the weightiness of the judgment we deserve that we can have any appreciation for the grace we do not deserve. Likewise, it is only after we become aware of the extent of our treachery that we can value forgiveness as we should.

Jeremiah began to comprehend the extent of Israel's betrayal. After all, even his own family had betrayed him. He could now begin to see that judgment was indeed necessary, and this had prepared him for the next lesson—God's glorious mercy:

- "I will send disaster upon the leaders of my people—the shepherds of my sheep—for they have destroyed and scattered the very ones they were expected to care for," says the LORD. This is what the LORD, the God of Israel, says to these shepherds: "Instead of leading my flock to safety, you have deserted them and driven them to destruction. Now I will pour out judgment on you for the evil you have done to them. But I will gather together the remnant of my flock from wherever I have driven them. I will bring them back into their own fold, and they will be fruitful and increase in number. Then I will appoint responsible shepherds to care for them, and they will never be afraid again. Not a single one of them will be lost or missing," says the LORD. "For the time is coming," says the LORD, "when I will place a righteous Branch on King David's throne. He will be a King who rules with wisdom. He will do what is just and right throughout the land. And this is his name: 'The LORD Is Our Righteousness'" (Jeremiah 23:1-6).

It is from the darkness of rebellion and judgment that Messiah is best seen for who He is. Our Lord is most fully embraced and understood through a veil of tears and desperation. As the hurricane precedes the rainbow, the bad news must precede the good. The reality of our deserved judgment must serve as the herald for grace. And finally, we must suffer with Christ so that we can reign with Him. There are certain truths that we must first learn the hard way, even as Jeremiah had to learn them.

❖ ❖ ❖

Moving on from Jeremiah, I wonder...could it be that all of the prophets had a problem with God?

In Ezekiel 7, God had announced to the prophet the destruction of Judah and Jerusalem. Ezekiel must have been rocked to the core of his being by this revelation. In Ezekiel 8, in order to justify His coming judgment, the Lord took Ezekiel—in the Spirit—to see the abominations that the leaders were committing in the Temple. Yet—understandably—Ezekiel was still appalled by the coming judgment:

- So it was, that while they were killing them [Israel], I was left alone; and I fell on my face and cried out, and said, "Ah, Lord GOD! Will you destroy all the remnant of Israel in pouring out your fury on Jerusalem?" (Ezekiel 9:8; see also 11:13)

Responding to His prophet, God revealed the Messianic mercy that would one day come:

- "Therefore say, 'Thus says the Lord GOD: I will gather you from the peoples and assemble you out of the countries where you have been scattered, and I will give you the land of Israel.' And when they come there, they will remove from it all its detestable things and all its abominations. And I will give them one heart, and a new spirit I will put within them. I will remove the heart of stone from their flesh and give them a heart of flesh, that they may walk in my statutes and keep my rules and obey them. And they shall be my people, and I will be their God." (Ezekiel 11:17-20)

Ezekiel first had to hear the bad news before he could appreciate the Good News!

❖ ❖ ❖

The prophet Habakkuk also had a problem with God. Habakkuk had complained to God about the violence he had been observing in Judah. God had the remedy for the situation: He would bring the Babylonians against Judah to destroy them! Once again, and quite understandably, the prophet was shocked:

- "You are of purer eyes than to behold evil, and cannot look on wickedness. Why do You look on those who deal treacherously, and hold Your tongue when the wicked [Babylon] devours a person more righteous than he?" (Habakkuk 1:13)

Habakkuk's words compel us to ask a question: Was Judah indeed more righteous than Babylon? Again, it would be good for us to remember that we have a tendency to think more of our own people than we sometimes should. We tend to give those in our own "tribe" the benefit of any doubt. However, God assured Habakkuk that His judgment would not be indiscriminate. Instead, in words that are familiar to our ears, the Lord declared to Habakkuk that "the righteous shall live by faith" (Habakkuk 2:4).

In the same way, God also assured Ezekiel of the mercy that He would show to those who were repentant:

- And the LORD said to him [an angelic being], "Pass through the city, through Jerusalem, and put a mark on the foreheads of the men who sigh and groan over all the abominations that are committed in it." And to the others he said in my hearing, "Pass through the city after him, and strike. Your eye shall not spare, and you shall show no pity." (Ezekiel 9:4-5)

God knows those who are His, and He will bring judgment on those who are not. This revelation enabled Habakkuk to close his book with his famous prayer of praise:

- Though the fig tree should not blossom, nor fruit be on the vines, the produce of the olive fail and the fields yield no food, the flock be cut off from the fold and there be no herd in the stalls, yet I will rejoice in the LORD; I will take joy in the God of my salvation. GOD, the Lord, is my strength; he makes my feet like the deer's; he makes me tread on my high places. (Habakkuk 3:17-19)

❖ ❖ ❖

The prophet Jonah had such a serious problem with the Word of God that he fled! He would have gladly given up his life to avoid bringing God's Word of warning to Nineveh, a city which he found utterly contemptible. Since Jonah was not yet ready to listen to God's call, the Lord sent a great fish who was able to "preach" a message to Jonah that he could not refuse. While he was imprisoned in the fish's belly, Jonah received God's message and prayed:

- "When my life was fainting away, I remembered the LORD, and my prayer came to you, into your holy temple...But I with the voice of thanksgiving will sacrifice to you; what I have vowed I will pay. Salvation belongs to the LORD!" (Jonah 2:7, 9)

Jonah freely acknowledged that salvation belongs to the LORD. Furthermore, he accepted the fact that God could grant the gift of His salvation to whomever He chose—even to the hated, ruthless Assyrians. Once Jonah had come to this understanding, the fish spit him up onto a beach adjacent to Nineveh, where Jonah began to preach:

- Then the word of the LORD came to Jonah the second time, saying, "Arise, go to Nineveh, that great city, and call out against it the message that I tell you." So Jonah arose and went to Nineveh, according to the word of the LORD. Now Nineveh was an exceedingly great city, three days' journey in breadth. Jonah began to go into the city, going a day's journey. And he called out, "Yet forty days, and Nineveh shall be overthrown!" (Jonah 3:1-4)

When the people of Nineveh repented at God's warning through His prophet, Jonah's greatest fear was realized:

- When God saw what they [the Assyrians] did and how they turned from their evil ways, he had compassion and did not bring upon them the destruction he had threatened. (Jonah 3:10)

Jonah knew that God's promise to bring destruction on the city of Nineveh was conditional and depended on Nineveh's response. He had such a hatred for Nineveh that he would have been glad to deliver a message proclaiming Nineveh's unconditional destruction. However, Jonah also knew that God might relent, and that is why he had fled. He did not want to preach a message that might have led to Nineveh's repentance. He complained:

- "O LORD, is this not what I said when I was still at home? That is why I was so quick to flee to Tarshish. I knew that you are a gracious and compassionate God, slow to anger and abounding in love, a God who relents from sending calamity." (Jonah 4:1-2)

God was not finished with Jonah. As He desires for all of His people, God wanted Jonah to be more than a simple robotic mouthpiece for Him. God wanted Jonah to be a willing participant in His plans. In the same way, He wants each of us to understand Him and worship Him in spirit and in truth (John 4:22-24). Therefore, for Jonah's second object lesson, God would reason with him, not with a fish—but with a plant!

This plant had provided Jonah with shade, but it suddenly died. And Jonah was furious:

- But God said to Jonah, "Do you do well to be angry for the plant?" And he said, "Yes, I do well to be angry, angry enough to die." And the LORD said, "You pity the plant, for which you did not labor, nor did you make it grow, which came into being in a night and perished in a night. And should not I pity Nineveh, that great city, in which there are more than 120,000 persons who do not know their right hand from their left, and also much cattle?" (Jonah 4:9-11)

Jonah's problem with God was with His grace to those that Jonah regarded as less deserving. However, God reasoned that if Jonah pitied the plant, He had far more reason to pity 120,000 people who had been rescued from destruction.

Jonah needed this object lesson and so do I. In order for me to learn mercy towards others, I had to first painfully learn about my need for God's mercy. In my totally unjustified self-confidence, I had attempted to set up a Christian counseling agency. I had no clue about all that was involved in such a venture. As a result, I made an absolute mess out of everything. My only client felt compelled to flee from my office!

After this, I had to learn about the absolute certainty of God's mercy for the broken-hearted. Only then could I begin to serve my Savior faithfully.

Chapter 12

UNDERSTANDING ISAIAH'S PROBLEM WITH GOD

CHAPTER SUMMARY

Should all Israel be saved? The prophet Isaiah declared that God is the Potter and Israel, the clay. How is it, then, that God could not mold Israel into righteousness?

Isaiah did not seem to have any illusions about Israel's merit or righteousness. If he ever leaned in that direction, God promptly brought him up short:

- Hear, O heavens, and give ear, O earth; for the LORD has spoken: "Children have I reared and brought up, but they have rebelled against me. The ox knows its owner, and the donkey its master's crib, but Israel does not know, my people do not understand." Ah, sinful nation, a people laden with iniquity, offspring of evildoers, children who deal corruptly! They have forsaken the LORD, they have despised the Holy One of Israel, they are utterly estranged. (Isaiah 1:2-4)

Isaiah was well aware that Israel was not without guilt. At the same time, Isaiah understood that God is omnipotent and could do anything He wanted to do:

- All of us have become like one who is unclean, and all our righteous acts are like filthy rags; we all shrivel up like a leaf, and like the wind our sins sweep us away. No one calls on your name or strives to lay hold of you; for you have hidden your face from us and made us waste away because of our sins. *Yet, O LORD, you are our*

> *Father. We are the clay, you are the potter; we are all the work of your hand.* (Isaiah 64:6-8, emphasis added)

Yes, Isaiah knew that Israel was rebellious and deserved judgment. However, if God is the Potter, then shouldn't He be able to mold Israel into a righteous nation?

- Do not be angry beyond measure, O LORD; do not remember our sins forever. Oh, look upon us, we pray, for we are all your people…After all this, O LORD, will you hold yourself back? Will you keep silent and punish us beyond measure? (Isaiah 64:9,12)

Isaiah was perplexed. The LORD was holding Himself back from changing His people! God's answer to the questions of His prophet must have been less than satisfying:

- "All day long I have held out my hands to an obstinate people, who walk in ways not good, pursuing their own imaginations—a people who continually provoke me to my very face, offering sacrifices in gardens and burning incense on altars of brick [to false gods]…I will destine you for the sword, and you will all bend down for the slaughter; for I called but you did not answer, I spoke but you did not listen. You did evil in my sight and chose what displeases me." (Isaiah 65:2-3,12)

This is not a direct answer to Isaiah's question. And yet, in many ways, He had already given His answer. After all, hadn't God already given His beloved Israel everything? And what was He given in return?

- Let me sing for my beloved my love song concerning his vineyard: My beloved had a vineyard on a very fertile hill. He dug it and cleared it of stones, and planted it with choice vines; he built a watchtower in the midst of it, and hewed out a wine vat in it; and he looked for it to yield grapes, but it yielded wild grapes. And now, O inhabitants of Jerusalem and men of Judah, judge between me and my vineyard. What more was there to do for my vineyard, that I have not done in it? When I looked for it to yield grapes, why did it yield wild grapes? (Isaiah 5:1-4)

And so it is clear: God did not hold back anything from His people, as Isaiah had suggested. However, if God is omnipotent, then this is hard for us to understand. If He had changed the heart of some Israelites, why could He not change the heart of all of them?

These issues necessarily lead us to look more deeply into God's omnipotence. Can He indeed do anything? Actually, this does not seem to be the case. While He can accomplish anything He wants, there are certain things that He cannot do. One such thing He absolutely cannot do is sin. This would be a total violation of His character. Nor does it seem as if He could violate His promises. Perhaps He is also unable to violate His internal logic and create a stone He could not lift.

Let us take a look at something that happened in the life of Christ that might help us here. In Jesus' prayer in the Garden of Gethsemane, something that He said sheds light on the idea of the Father's Self-limitation:

- Going a little farther, he [Jesus] fell with his face to the ground and prayed, "My Father, if it is possible, may this cup [the Cross] be taken from me. Yet not as I will, but as you will." (Matthew 26:39)

While God can do all things, He cannot do them *in any manner whatsoever.* He was not able to grant Jesus His request. God's righteous character prevented the payment for the sins of humanity in any other way than the death of His Son. Jesus had to die. The sacrifice of any number of animals would certainly not have been able to purchase our forgiveness. Thus, we can see that there are some limitations concerning what God can do.

Let us now apply this to the issue of God saving all Israel. While we know, according to 2 Peter 3:9, that God wants everyone to be saved, there might be a Self-limitation within His Nature that does not permit this. If the Father was not able to grant Jesus' request, perhaps there is also something that prevents Him from saving and transforming all people—or at least, saving all Israel, as Isaiah had requested.

Nevertheless, God did answer Isaiah with a promise that He would show incredible grace to Israel—but only through the Messiah:

- "The Redeemer [the promised Messiah] will come to Zion, to those in Jacob who repent of their sins," declares the LORD. "As for me, this is my covenant with them," says the LORD. "My Spirit, who is on you, and my words that I have put in your mouth will not depart from your mouth, or from the mouths of your children, or from the mouths of their descendants from this time on and forever," says the LORD. (Isaiah 59:20-21)

- "Behold, I will create new heavens and a new earth. The former things will not be remembered, nor will they come to mind. But be glad and rejoice forever in what I will create, for I will create Jerusalem to be a delight and its people a joy. I will rejoice over Jerusalem and take delight in my people; the sound of weeping and of crying will be heard in it no more." (Isaiah 65:17-19)

God has promised a new world of "delight," which will last forever. In the end, there will be a great salvation. After the final battle, all those who are left will be rescued:

- "From one New Moon to another and from one Sabbath to another, all mankind will come and bow down before me," says the LORD. (Isaiah 66:23)

This is an indication that, in the end, our Lord will open the floodgates of heaven:

- "Turn to me and be saved, all you ends of the earth; for I am God, and there is no other...Before me every knee will bow; by me every tongue will swear. They will say of me, 'In the LORD alone are righteousness and strength.'" All who have raged against him will come to him and be put to shame. But in the LORD all the descendants of Israel will be found righteous and will exult. (Isaiah 45:22, 23b-25; see also Isaiah 60:14; Romans 11:12-27; James 2:13.)

But...God made all of us the way we are, right? Then, is the Potter not also to blame for the way the work of His hands turns out? This is one charge that the prophets never brought against God. Instead, they accepted what He had revealed—that the fault is all ours, and that God had done for Israel everything He could have done (Isaiah 5:2-5; Jeremiah 2:21).

Isaiah's charge against God was merely that He *could have* corrected Israel's heart. However, it must be admitted that Isaiah probably never received a complete and satisfactory answer. Perhaps what God had revealed to him was enough.

Hopefully, it will be enough for us, at least for the time being.

Chapter 13

UNDERSTANDING ISAIAH'S PROPHECY OF THE VIRGIN BIRTH

CHAPTER SUMMARY

"Behold, the virgin shall be with child, and bear a Son, and they shall call His name Immanuel," which is translated, "God with us" (Matthew 1:23, quoting Isaiah 7:14). Deep study of this verse is eminently challenging but most worthy of our efforts to understand it.

Arguably, Isaiah 7:14, prophesying a virgin giving birth, is the most contested verse in the Old Testament. Although Matthew unequivocally states that this prophecy was fulfilled by the birth of the Messiah, the Old Testament seems to indicate that there was a fulfillment during the life of King Ahaz. Although this might appear to be a contradiction, these two perspectives can be reconciled using the understanding of a "double fulfillment." In other words, it was fulfilled initially for King Ahaz, and then it was fulfilled decisively through the birth of Jesus.

The Book of Matthew requires us to understand Isaiah 7:14 as a prophecy fulfilled by the birth of the Messiah Jesus to the virgin, Mary. However, the rabbis raise four potent challenges against this interpretation:

1. There is no imperative to take *Immanuel*—"God with us," in the Hebrew—as a description of "the child." Instead, rabbinical scholars insist that "Immanu*el*" is merely a name like Dani*el* or Nathani*el*. *El* always means "God" in Hebrew but is not necessarily a description of the nature

of the person.

2. The rabbis correctly assert that the Hebrew word *almah*, translated as "virgin" in Isaiah 7:14, can possibly be translated as "young maiden." Furthermore, if Isaiah had wanted to unequivocally portray the idea of "virgin," he could have used the unequivocal word, *betulah*, which always means "virgin."

3. The prophecy of Isaiah 7:14 was given to King Ahaz at around 735 BC. It was meant to be a divine sign for what God had promised him: that the two northern kings, Pekah (Israel) and Rezin (Syria)—who were threatening his own nation of Judah—would soon be destroyed, according to Isaiah 7:1-16. Thus, the birth of Jesus, which took place over 700 years later, could not possibly have been a sign meant for Ahaz.

4. Isaiah's prophecy seems to have been fulfilled by the birth of the prophet's own son. Isaiah had prophesied to Ahaz that the promised demise of Damascus (Syria) and Samaria (the Northern kingdom of Israel) would precede the promised child's maturation:

   - "Curds and honey He shall eat, that He may know to refuse the evil and choose the good. For *before* the Child shall know to refuse the evil and choose the good, the land that you dread will be forsaken by both her kings." (Isaiah 7:15-16, emphasis added)

This same prophecy seems to be repeated shortly thereafter, when Isaiah's wife gives birth to their own child, Maher-Shalal-Hash-Baz:

   - "Then I [Isaiah] went to the prophetess, and she conceived and bore a son. Then the Lord said to me, 'Call his name Maher-Shalal-Hash-Baz; for *before* the child shall have knowledge to cry 'My father' and 'My mother,' the riches of Damascus and the spoil of Samaria will be taken away before the king of Assyria.'" (Isaiah 8:3-4, emphasis added)

Once again, in both of these prophecies, we can see that the destruction of Damascus and Samaria would precede the child's maturation. This seems to indicate that the prophecy had already been fulfilled with the birth of Isaiah's son, 700 years before Christ. Therefore, there are some who hold that Christian scholars who apply this prophecy to the birth of Christ have illegitimately manipulated the Hebrew Scriptures into saying what it never intended to say. Thus, these same people make the very serious charge that Christianity has hidden itself behind some very imaginative and self-serving speculations.

❖ ❖ ❖

Let's start with the last challenge first. If the birth of Isaiah's son had already fulfilled Isaiah 7:14, then this is a clear case of a multiple fulfillment—a single prophetic message fulfilled at different times and in different ways. When such multiple fulfillments occur, the ultimate fulfillments are often preceded by types, foreshadowings, or symbols. This is clearly visible in the New Testament, which understands the entire sacrificial system—with its holidays and offerings—as a foreshadowing of Christ, the ultimate fulfillment.

But do the Hebrew Scriptures also provide evidence for this type of foreshadowing—that some prophecies and objects often serve as pre-figurings or types of ultimate realities yet to be revealed? Yes! Although the Hebrew Scriptures are not often explicit about pointing out types, they nevertheless do allude to them.

For example, the prophet Zechariah saw the broken, assailed high priest Joshua as a type of the One to come:

- Then he showed me Joshua the high priest standing before the Angel of the LORD, and Satan standing at his right hand to oppose him. And the LORD said to Satan, "The LORD rebuke you, Satan! The LORD who has chosen Jerusalem rebuke you! Is this not a brand plucked from the fire?" Now Joshua was clothed with filthy garments, and was standing before the Angel. Then He answered and spoke to those who stood before Him, saying, "Take away the filthy garments from him." And to him He said, "See, I have removed your iniquity from you, and I will clothe you with rich robes." And I said, "Let them put a clean turban on his head." So they put a clean turban on his head, and they put the clothes on him. And the Angel of the LORD stood by...
  'Hear, O Joshua, the high priest,
  You and your companions who sit before you,
  For they are a wondrous sign;
  For behold, I am bringing forth My Servant the BRANCH.
  For behold, the stone
  That I have laid before Joshua:
  Upon the stone are seven eyes.
  Behold, I will engrave its inscription,'
  Says the LORD of hosts,
  'And I will remove the iniquity of that land in one day.'"
  (Zechariah 3:1-5; 8-9, emphasis added)

This passage abounds in pre-figurings and types. Joshua and his companions are symbolic of what the Lord will ultimately do through the Messiah. The filthy garments are symbolic of the sins that God will remove "in one day." This removal serves as a foreshadowing of a justification by grace through faith alone. After all, Joshua was certainly sin-stained. God never corrected the damning accusations of Satan. They were probably true, but our righteous God did something Satan could never understand. Just as Joshua's filthy garments were removed, God would remove sin through the undisclosed work of a mysterious individual, "the BRANCH."

The identity of the Branch becomes clearer three chapters later. There, we see that Zechariah was given another assignment regarding Joshua in his symbolic role:

- "Take the silver and gold, make an elaborate crown, and set it on the head of Joshua the son of Jehozadak, the high priest. Then speak to him, saying, 'Thus says the LORD of hosts, saying: 'Behold, the Man whose name is the BRANCH! From His place He shall branch out, and He shall build the temple of the LORD. Yes, He shall build the temple of the LORD. He shall bear the glory, and shall sit and rule on His throne; so He shall be a priest on His throne.'" **(Zechariah 6:11-13).**

This passage is also replete with types and symbols. A crown is placed upon the head of Joshua, ostensibly making this priest a king. However, Joshua never actually became a king, nor was he supposed to be. Israel already had a civil magistrate, Zerubbabel. If Joshua had become king, this would have brought him into direct conflict with Zerubbabel. Besides, we have no evidence that this ever happened. From all indications, the two leaders worked together in harmony to build the Temple.

Furthermore, a separation of powers had been strictly instituted in Israel. A priest could not become a king, and a king could not become a priest. Only the Messiah would be worthy enough to occupy both of these posts (Psalm 110). Through the symbolism related to Joshua, God was revealing the way in which He would ultimately bring the two offices together…through the glorious Branch, who would "sit and rule on His throne." Thus, Joshua was merely a type or pre-figuring of Someone greater, who would ultimately fulfill the type.

❖ ❖ ❖

Are we confronted with something similar in Isaiah 7? Could Isaiah's own child be a sign of a more glorious Child? Here is what Isaiah said:

- "Here am I and the children whom the LORD has given me! *We are for signs and wonders in Israel* from the LORD of hosts, who dwells in Mount Zion." (Isaiah 8:18, emphasis added)

How were Isaiah and his children "signs and wonders"? Could Maher-Shalal-Hash-Baz have prefigured the Messiah, as Joshua did? The narratives regarding Joshua clearly point to a Person beyond Joshua. Does the Isaiah passage point beyond Isaiah's son? To answer these questions, it is imperative that we regard the broader context of Chapters 7-12 of Isaiah, where we find the same elements of the "Immanuel" prophecy repeated. These related narratives serve to put flesh and bones on the original prophecy.

The term "Immanuel" is a conjunction of two very common words: *Immanu,* translated as "with us," and *El,* meaning "God." It appears only three times in Hebrew Scripture. The first instance is found in Isaiah 7:14. The other two instances are both found in the next chapter. This alone would suggest that the three instances are related in Isaiah's mind—and, I believe, in the mind of God. Additionally, all three uses are unusual, provocative, and thematically connected.

We encounter the word "Immanuel" for the second time after Isaiah describes what Assyria will do to Judah after Assyria swallows up Syria ("Damascus" or "Aram") and the northern kingdom of Israel ("Ephraim") in 721 BC.

- "Now therefore, behold, the Lord brings up over them the waters of the River, strong and mighty—the king of Assyria and all his glory; he will go up over all his channels and go over all his banks. He will pass through Judah, he will overflow and pass over, he will reach up to the neck [Jerusalem]; and the stretching out of his wings will fill the breadth of *Your* land, O *Immanuel*" [translated, "God with us"]. (Isaiah 8:7-8, emphasis added).

Thus we can see that Assyria would conquer Judah, but only "up to the neck." This probably refers to Assyria's unsuccessful siege of Jerusalem in 701 BC, which was terminated when the Angel of the Lord "put to death 185,000 men in the Assyrian camp" (Isaiah 37:36). Isaiah's prophecy ends with the ejaculation, "O Immanuel," seemingly an outcry for help to the exact same individual found in Isaiah 7:14. However, in this latter context, "Immanuel" seems to have been more than a mere man. After all, only God could have rescued Jerusalem, surrounded as she was by the mighty Assyrian army! It would have been ridiculous to cry out for help to any human being in such a hopeless situation. Assyria's victory had seemed absolutely assured; that is, short of miraculous intervention. And it was this divine intervention that turned the tide.

The third context where we find "Immanuel" is even more striking. In the next two verses, Isaiah 8:9-10, a warning is issued against Assyria and the nations it had overwhelmed and incorporated:

- "Be shattered, O you peoples, and be broken in pieces! Give ear, all you from far countries. Gird yourselves, but be broken in pieces; gird yourselves, but be broken in pieces. Take counsel together, but it will come to nothing; speak the word, but it will not stand, for *God is with us*" ["Immanuel" in the Hebrew]. (Isaiah 8:9-10, emphasis added)

Despite the overwhelming superiority of the Assyrian army, it would not succeed against the wobbling and panic-stricken Jerusalem, "the neck" of Isaiah 8:8. And the reason? "God is with us," the third instance where we encounter "Immanuel"! What started out as a cry for help in Isaiah 8:8 was transformed into a declaration of triumph in 8:10. "Immanuel" is clearly the cause of this triumph.

When we read the account of the destruction of the Assyrian army in Isaiah 36-39, it is clear that "Immanuel" cannot refer to Hezekiah, nor to any other mere mortal. "Immanuel" is appropriately translated here as "God is with us." He holds the destiny of nations in His hands. It is interesting to note that English translations of these verses understandably render the Hebrew as "God is with us," rather than simply "Immanuel," which consistency among the two prior instances would ordinarily demand. These translators correctly understood that it would be God Himself who would oppose Assyria.

To suggest that these three "Immanuels" represent three different people is more than sound interpretation will bear, especially since they are all found in the same biblical proximity. The more natural interpretation demands that the same titles or names pertain to the same person, who is both human—"a child"—and divine. In other words, this is none other than God Himself!

❖ ❖ ❖

The very familiar idea of the birth of a child found in Isaiah 7:14 is also repeated within the context of Chapters 7-12 and serves to unify this whole portion of the Book of Isaiah:

- "For unto us a Child is born, unto us a Son is given; and the government will be upon His shoulder. And His name will be called Wonderful, Counselor, Mighty God, Everlasting Father, Prince of Peace. Of the increase of His government and peace there will be no end, upon the throne of David and over His kingdom, to order it and establish it with judgment and justice from that time forward, even forever..." **(Isaiah 9:6-7a)**.

This prophecy is not only related to 7:14 by virtue of the birth of a special child, but also by the divine names that are mentioned. In 7:14, we encounter a divine name or description designating a child. In 9:6 we encounter four divine titles. I choose to write "titles" here because the words used are not really names but descriptive titles of this child. Furthermore, the four titles contain eight words—too cumbersome for actual names. It would be like naming a newborn "Anthony Robert Spencer Alan Thomas Arthur Andrew Timothy." Such a lengthy name is without precedent in the Bible. Instead, we understand these eight words as descriptions of the identity of the child.

The first title, "Wonderful Counselor"—*Pele Yoetz* in Hebrew—is clearly divine. *Pele* might better have been translated "awesome" because this term only refers to God or to the wonders He miraculously brings into existence (Exodus 15:11; Daniel 12:6).

"Mighty God"—*El Gibor*—is also clearly a divine title because *El,* as a free-standing word, always refers to God. In addition to this, we should notice that *Immanu El* of 7:14 also carries the free-standing *El*—as is the case in 8:8 and 8:10—establishing another parallel with 7:14. This also serves to rule against *Immanu El* as merely being a name, as the rabbis propose, instead of a description.

"Everlasting Father" is also a divine designation. Who can be everlasting apart from God Himself? Even "Prince of Peace" seems to be a divine reference, for it is God Himself who brings peace, according to Leviticus 26:6, Numbers 6:26 and Numbers 25:12. Jewish interpreters choose to understand these divine names as mere reminders that it is God who is performing His works through this child. However, it is this very Child who is called these descriptive titles. Nowhere does the text suggest that

He is given these divine titles *in remembrance of God!*

It strains credulity to say that the Child of Isaiah 9:6 is different from the Child of Isaiah 7:14. As the *Immanu El* of Isaiah 7:14 will reign supreme, so too will the *El Gibor* of Isaiah 9:6. Are we looking at two reigning Deities, or at one? The Child of Isaiah 9:6 will set up a kingdom with no end. This leaves little room for any other divine children or kingdoms. There can only be One!

❖ ❖ ❖

Our discussion here would not be complete without mentioning Isaiah 11, where we find yet another allusion to the Child:

- "There shall come forth a Rod from the stem of Jesse, and a Branch shall grow out of his roots. The Spirit of the LORD shall rest upon Him, the Spirit of wisdom and understanding, the Spirit of counsel and might, the Spirit of knowledge and of the fear of the LORD. His delight is in the fear of the LORD, and He shall not judge by the sight of His eyes, nor decide by the hearing of His ears; but with righteousness He shall judge the poor, and decide with equity for the meek of the earth; He shall strike the earth with the rod of His mouth, and with the breath of His lips He shall slay the wicked. Righteousness shall be the belt of His loins, and faithfulness the belt of His waist. The wolf also shall dwell with the lamb…They shall not hurt nor destroy in all My holy mountain, for the earth shall be full of the knowledge of the LORD as the waters cover the sea." (Isaiah 11:1-6a, 9)

Here we discover an enlargement of the portrait established earlier. We find the Child, at long last, reigning in His own kingdom. He is a "Rod" and a "Branch," born from the "stump of Jesse," the father of King David. Unmistakably, this is the same Child who "will reign upon the throne of David and over his kingdom" (Isaiah 9:7).

Other parallels are also clear. The kingdoms cited in both Isaiah 9:7 and 11:9 "will have no end." Both kingdoms will entail the establishment of "justice and righteousness," found in 9:6 and 11:3-5. In addition, the idea of endless "peace" may be found in both 9:7 and 11:6-9. Therefore, we can say with the utmost confidence that the same kingdom is on view in both chapters.

These chapters also build upon one another. In addition to the above elaborations on the initial prophetic germ, the four divine titles of 9:6 and the fifth from 7:14 seem to receive an expanded treatment in Isaiah 11: "Wonderful Counselor" in verses 2-5 and "Prince of Peace" in verses 6-9. Perhaps *El Gibor* and "Everlasting Father" are reflected within the entire prophecy of Chapter 11 and the prayer of Chapter 12.

The parallels we have discussed here demonstrate that these prophecies are closely related. If this is the case, then one prophecy is illuminated and enhanced by the others. We must try to understand *Immanu El* and the "child" of 7:14 in a way that accords with the subsequent prophecies in Chapters 8, 9, and 11. The seed of a prophecy that Isaiah proclaimed in 7:14, and which was enlarged upon in 8:6-10 and again in 9:6-7, is proclaimed boldly in Chapter 11. This Child is indeed the cause of all the world's rejoicing!

It is only natural that this great revelation should culminate in the song of praise found in Chapter 12. This song of Isaiah has several interesting characteristics. There are three references to "salvation"—*Yeshua* in the Hebrew—calling to mind Jesus' likely Hebrew name:

- "Behold, God is *my salvation*, I will trust and not be afraid; for YAH, the LORD, is my strength and song; He also has become *my salvation*. Therefore with joy you will draw water from the wells of *salvation*." (Isaiah 12:2-3, emphasis added)

In addition, we should note that Chapter 12 concludes in v. 6 with "the Holy One of Israel *in your midst*." This seems to be a play on the similar *Immanu El*, "God with us." The words are different but the idea portrayed is the same. All of this suggests that Chapters 7-12 need to be regarded together, as an inseparable prophetic utterance.

If Isaiah 7:14 is indeed part of a greater prophecy found in Isaiah 7-12, then this verse must be understood within that entire unified setting. Any word or phrase needs the full context of the sentence, paragraph or even whole section of the writing in which it occurs to be truly understood. Understanding *Immanu El* as merely a human child who was born during the reign of King Ahaz fails to correctly interpret Isaiah 7:14 in its broader context. This is an interpretive failure that an unbiased eye would not allow.

Many years before the advent of the Christ, the rabbis translated the Hebrew Bible, including Isaiah, into Greek for the Jews of the Diaspora. In the course of their work, they obviously needed to confront Isaiah 7:14. If *almah* was a word that was equivocal and could be translated by either "virgin" or "young maiden," the rabbis had an important choice to make. If they translated it as "young maiden," it meant that they understood that the prophecy had been fulfilled *in its totality* at the time of Ahaz. If they translated *almah* as "virgin," then they understood that the word was referring to a miraculous birth that had not yet taken place, a fulfillment which was still awaiting its day. They decided to translate *almah* as *parthenos* in the Greek, a term that unequivocally means "virgin"! In light of this, Matthew, quoting Isaiah, was simply thinking in the same state of prophetic expectancy as these rabbis when he applied this prophecy to the birth of the Messiah, *Yeshua*.

❖ ❖ ❖

Let's return now to the third objection of the rabbis—that the birth of Jesus, or *Yeshua*, could not possibly have been a sign for Ahaz, to whom the prophecy was addressed. However, a closer look at the text shows that *the prophecy was not intended for Ahaz alone*. The entire "house of David" was in view:

- "Then he said, 'Hear now, O *house of David!* Is it a small thing for you to weary men, but will you weary my God also? Therefore the Lord Himself will give you [plural] a sign: Behold, the virgin shall conceive and bear a Son, and shall call His name Immanuel.'" (7:13-14, emphasis added)

Isaiah recognized that the audience for his prophecy went beyond Ahaz. His message transcended its temporal boundaries, and he knew it. It is clear that the prophecies of Isaiah constitute a sign of something far greater. Let us examine this pertinent verse yet again:

- "Here am I and the children whom the LORD has given me! *We are for signs and wonders in Israel* from the LORD of hosts, who dwells in Mount Zion." (Isaiah 8:18, emphasis added)

There is still another reason why neither Hezekiah nor Isaiah's son could have fulfilled Isaiah 7:14 in its entirety. After all, a natural birth is hardly a sign or a symbol. Young women give birth all the time. There is nothing unusual about this, nothing that would have the persuasive weight to confirm a seemingly improbable prophecy. Only an unusual birth—a virgin birth—would constitute a legitimate sign.

Clearly, this prophecy reaches beyond the person and time of Ahaz. In many ways, it points to a divine Person standing at the headwaters of history, a Person who holds the destiny of Israel in His hands. In the strongest terms, this particular prophecy cries out that this is the One for whom Israel had been waiting. This is the One who, according to Isaiah 9:7, would fulfill all the promises of God while seated on "David's throne." Again, from Isaiah 9:7, we know that it would be this Child who would set up an everlasting kingdom where the peace would never end. From Isaiah 11:9, we know that "the earth will be full of the knowledge of the LORD as the waters cover the sea." Although there was a type or a shadow of fulfillment in Ahaz's time, the ultimate fulfillment of Isaiah 7:14 awaited the Messiah.

I have a Jewish friend who believes that Jesus is the prophesied Messiah, but he is very conflicted in his understanding of the Messianic prophecies. This lack of understanding robs him of peace. The antidote for the conflict that rages in so many of us is *a rational resolution of the conflict*. This requires persistent work, but even more than work, the grace of God is essential. Thankfully, He promises to pour out His grace liberally upon every weary soul who seeks His wisdom.

- The LORD confides in those who fear him; he makes his covenant known to them. (Psalm 25:14)

- Surely you desire truth in the inner parts; you teach me wisdom in the inmost place. (Psalm 51:6)

- If any of you lacks wisdom, he should ask God, who gives generously to all without finding fault, and it will be given to him. (James 1:5)

I must apologize for this mentally demanding chapter. However, I wouldn't have included it if it wasn't of the gravest importance in this embattled controversy. Perhaps even more importantly, meditating on these gleanings from Isaiah can elevate our contemplations to the very seat of glory.

Chapter 14

UNDERSTANDING TROUBLING PASSAGES OF THE HEBREW SCRIPTURES

CHAPTER SUMMARY

The Hebrew Scriptures represent God's wisdom in accommodating to Israelite culture and to their spiritual needs.

There are many things in the Old Testament that are perplexing and even troubling. For example, in Numbers 35:19-29, we discover the duties and description of "the avenger of blood." Today we might refer to this person as a bounty hunter! What about the divine allowances for polygamy and slavery? And let us not forget the destruction of the Canaanites.

How do we reconcile these practices with the teachings of the New Testament, or with our modern intuitions regarding justice? Richard F. Lovelace explains this tension through the need to "disenculturate" Israel from the culture of Egypt and from the various Canaanite cultures:

- One of the first effects of spiritual decline among the people of God is destructive enculturation, saturation with the godless culture of the surrounding world as we saw in Judges 2:11-13. When men's hearts are not full of God, they become full of the world around like a sponge full of clear water that has been squeezed empty and thrown into a mud puddle. (Lovelace, Richard F. *Dynamics of Spiritual Life: An Evangelical Theology of Renewal.* IVP, 1981, p. 184)

How would Israel become "full of God"? Continuing to utilize his metaphor, Lovelace argues that if a sponge is soaked with oil, it will not absorb anything else. God therefore wanted to saturate Israel with His laws and rituals to such an extent that His people would not absorb anything from the surrounding cultures.

In many ways, Israel had not been eager to do this. Even though God had manifested His faithfulness to His people in so many ways, the Israelites had even gone so far as to worship a golden calf—an idol with which they had become familiar during their sojourn in Egypt:

- When the people saw that Moses delayed to come down from the mountain, the people gathered themselves together to Aaron and said to him, "Up, make us gods who shall go before us. As for this Moses, the man who brought us up out of the land of Egypt, we do not know what has become of him." (Exodus 32:1)

Later on in their history, the Israelites—so that they could be like the nations around them—demanded a king (1 Samuel 8:5). However, even though a king was not God's first choice for His people, Mosaic Law accommodated Israel's desires and demands. But, for the good of the nation, God declared that the choosing of kings was to be regulated by His guidelines. Furthermore, the king had to be careful to abide by the Law, just like all his subjects (Deuteronomy 17).

Israel also demanded divorce, which did not coincide with God's original plan for His people, as Jesus clearly taught. Instead, it was granted as a concession to Israel's hardened heart (Matthew 19:4-6). My guess is that, in the wisdom of God, He thought it would be better to allow His people to divorce rather than abuse one another.

To some degree, the Law was a concession to Israel's stubbornness. It would be good for us to remember this as we try to understand many of the prescribed institutions of Mosaic Law. Therefore, divorce, polygamy, the office of the avenger-of-blood, and many other practices were allowed by the Law but were also divinely regulated.

Because of the overwhelming desire of the Israelites to be like other nations, it seems as if Israel's prescribed rituals and offerings—at least superficially—resembled those of the surrounding cultures. Nevertheless, even though Israel's religion was not entirely different in form from those of its surrounding neighbors, according to 2 Timothy 3:16-17, it was still God-inspired in its entirety. Here is what Jesus had to say about the divine origins of the Law:

- "Do not think that I have come to abolish the Law or the Prophets; I have not come to abolish them but to fulfill them. I tell you the truth, until heaven and earth disappear, not the smallest letter, not the least stroke of a pen will by any means disappear from the Law until everything is accomplished." (Matthew 5:17-18)

There can be no doubt that Jesus considered the Law to be a gift from the hand of God to humanity. And yet, it seems as if the Mosaic system of blood offerings—to look at another example—was both God-breathed and also an accommodation to the desire of the Israelites to be like other nations. All of the countries surrounding Israel presented sacrificial offerings. However, the Mosaic offerings conveyed a different understanding. For one thing, even though God *required* them, He didn't really *esteem* them as the ultimate form of worship. Why not? The sacrifices offered by the priests of Israel were intended to point to something greater:

- For since the law has but a shadow of the good things to come instead of the true form of these realities, it can never, by the same sacrifices that are continually offered every year, make perfect those who draw near. Otherwise, would they not have ceased to be offered, since the worshipers, having once been cleansed, would no longer have any consciousness of sins? But in these sacrifices there is a reminder of sins every year. For it is impossible for the blood of bulls and goats to take away sins. Consequently, when Christ came into the world, he said, "Sacrifices and offerings you have not desired, but a body have you prepared for me; in burnt offerings and sin offerings you have taken no pleasure. Then I said, 'Behold, I have come to do your will, O God, as it is written of me in the scroll of the book.'" (Hebrews 10:1-7 quoting from Psalm 40)

God used His Law to point to the ultimate sacrifice—Jesus. The Mosaic Law is like a language using the same alphabet as other belief systems. However, the letters are arranged in a special way to convey an entirely different, unique message.

To take another example, we can see that the Israelite Temple was similar to its Egyptian counterpart. However, the way the Jerusalem Temple was arranged conveyed an unprecedented and distinct religious message. While the Egyptian temple contained cots for their gods, there was no such thing in the Israelite Temple. Thus, the idea being conveyed by the design of the Temple in Jerusalem was that God did not sleep there. His abode was far more expansive.

Once again we can see that, even though the Israelite Temple and its system of offerings in some ways reflected those of pagan cultures, they were, nevertheless, entirely a revelation of Israel's God. According to Romans 7:12, the Law was holy, and "the commandment is holy and righteous and good." Thus, the Law conveyed a divine revelation that was able to lead Israel to the grace that may be found in Christ:

- Before this faith came, we were held prisoners by the law, locked up until faith should be revealed. So the law was put in charge to lead us to Christ that we might be justified by faith. (Galatians 3:23-24)

In light of this truth, we can see that the Mosaic Covenant was just a temporary covenant until what the Bible refers to as "the fullness of time," when it would be replaced by the New Covenant:

- "The time is coming," declares the LORD, "when I will make a new covenant with the house of Israel and with the house of Judah...For I will forgive their wickedness and will remember their sins no more." (Jeremiah 31:31, 34b; see also Hosea 2:18-20)

As Paul so succinctly explained, for the Christian, there is no going back to the shadows, no returning to the Mosaic Law of the Old Testament:

- And you, who were dead in your trespasses and the uncircumcision of your flesh, God made alive together with him, having forgiven us all our trespasses, by canceling the record of debt that stood against us with its legal demands. This he set aside, nailing it to the cross...Therefore let no one pass judgment on you in questions of food and drink, or with regard to a festival or a new moon or a Sabbath. These are a shadow of the things to come, but the substance belongs to Christ. (Colossians 2:13-14, 16-17)

According to Peter in Acts 15:10, the Law was also "a yoke...that neither our fathers nor we have been able to bear." Therefore, Lovelace explains that...

- The message [of the OT] must therefore be disenculturated [from the OT culture], freed from its protective shell, so that it may take root in a thousand different cultural and political soils...The oil must be wrung out of the sponge, in order that it may be filled with [new] wine. (Lovelace, p. 186-87)

According to Lovelace, the sponge—Israel—filled with oil—the Law—had protected the Jewish nation from absorbing the religious oil from neighboring cultures. However, with the inauguration of the indwelling Holy Spirit through faith in Christ, Israel no longer needed the oil of the Law.

While the Pharisees continued to cherish the old wine of their transitory, impermanent Hebraic culture, Jesus argued that He had come with wine that was new, wine that had been prophesied in the OT. Therefore, He argued for new wineskins which would contain new wine—a new revelation. This new revelation would enable Christianity to spread abroad into other cultures that might have regarded the Mosaic culture as foreign and distasteful. The New Testament is like new wine that may be tasted and experienced in any culture. As the second-century *Epistle to Diognetus* described:

- For Christians cannot be distinguished from the rest of the human race by country, language or customs. They do not live in cities of their own; they do not use a peculiar form of speech; they do not follow an eccentric manner of life. (From B.J. Kidd, ed. *Documents Illustrative of the History of the Church*. Macmillan and Co., 1920)

While Christians should be able to be distinguished by their moral behavior, Diognetus pointed out that they had been free to take on the cultural trappings—wearing the clothes and speaking the language, for example—of whatever land in which they happened to live.

In summary, the Old Testament Law was an accommodation to the desires of Israel and the temptations posed by other cultures. At the same time, we recognize that the Mosaic Law is still completely the Word of God.

Chapter 15

UNDERSTANDING JESUS' TEACHINGS

CHAPTER SUMMARY

It is not easy to lay out a few rules that will enable us to accurately interpret the words of Christ. However, there are some guiding principles that are helpful. Jesus' full endorsement of the Hebrew Scriptures, along with the mandate to allow "Scripture to interpret Scripture," are of supreme importance.

Jesus' teachings are difficult. That is why we often avoid them. For one thing, Jesus taught in parables. In our Lord's own words, here is why:

- And the disciples came and said to Him, "Why do You speak to them in parables?" He answered and said to them, "Because it has been given to you to know the mysteries of the kingdom of heaven, but to them it has not been given. For whoever has, to him more will be given, and he will have abundance; but whoever does not have, even what he has will be taken away from him. Therefore I speak to them in parables, because seeing they do not see, and hearing they do not hear, nor do they understand." (Matthew 13:10-13)

This has allowed some people to twist Jesus' teachings to suit their own ends. Here is one common repudiation of Christianity from a guy we will call "Bob":

You Christians love to tell others how they're messing up, but you too refuse to follow Jesus!

When I asked Bob what he meant, this is what he said:

> *Jesus taught you to turn the other cheek, but you want to bomb the snot out of ISIS. Jesus taught you to give to anyone who asks, but you won't give me a miserable $20!*

These are serious charges. If Bob is right, then we who believe in Christ are hypocrites, telling others to follow Jesus while we ourselves conveniently neglect some of the things He said.

Let's take a look at one example of Jesus' teaching that deals with these issues:

- "But I tell you who hear me: Love your enemies, do good to those who hate you, bless those who curse you, pray for those who mistreat you. If someone strikes you on one cheek, turn to him the other also. If someone takes your cloak, do not stop him from taking your tunic. Give to everyone who asks you, and if anyone takes what belongs to you, do not demand it back." (Luke 6:27-30)

Are we literally to give to everyone who asks? Should I have given Bob the $20? Admittedly, this is a difficult set of verses to interpret. For one thing, it seems to contradict a number of other verses. But there is at least one thing we need to remember—the Apostle Paul taught explicitly that *we are not to give to everyone who asks*:

- For even when we were with you, we gave you this rule: "If a man will not work, he shall not eat." (2 Thessalonians 3:10)

If someone refuses to work, it would be wrong to support him. It would enable him to live in a counter-productive, dysfunctional way.

Jesus Himself taught that there are occasions when we should not give. We should not waste our pearls of wisdom on those who will turn against us (Matthew 7:6). Even Jesus did not give to everyone who asked of Him. On one occasion, James and John asked Jesus to make them His co-regents once He set up His kingdom. He turned them down!

Are we faced with a contradiction here, or is there a way for us to resolve it? There is a way! When Jesus spoke in parables, He would often use hyperbole—exaggerated language. Our attempts to understand Him must take this into account:

- "And if your right hand causes you to sin, cut it off and throw it away. It is better for you to lose one part of your body than for your whole body to go into hell." (Matthew 5:30)

No one takes this teaching literally. If we did, the Church would be full of people without hands! Likewise, no one takes Jesus' command to "pluck out your eye" literally (Matthew 5:29). However, His hyperbolic language makes a powerful point: If cutting off one's hand could keep someone from sin and Hell, then it would be a small price to pay.

But how can we be sure that Jesus was using hyperbole here? The answer is simple: Even if we did pluck out our eyes, it wouldn't prevent us from sinning. Recently, I read about a blind professional who left his wife for his secretary. Clearly, blindness is no cure for sin.

Parallel verses give us another way to detect hyperbole. Some verses are perplexing until we take into account how Jesus expressed the same thought in comparative verses. For example:

- "If anyone comes to me and does not hate his own father and mother and wife and children and brothers and sisters, yes, and even his own life, he cannot be my disciple." (Luke 14:26)

On the surface, this verse seems to contradict a number of biblical principles, like honoring one's parents. However, this problem is easily resolved when we observe a parallel teaching from Matthew:

- "Whoever loves father or mother more than me is not worthy of me, and whoever loves son or daughter more than me is not worthy of me." (Matthew 10:37)

The central issue here is a matter of priorities. Jesus must be our highest priority, even above ourselves and our family.

Here is another example of the same principle:

- "Do not think that I have come to bring peace to the earth. I have not come to bring peace, but a sword." (Matthew 10:34)

One skeptic tried to use this verse to prove that Jesus was teaching insurrection. However, we can easily counteract this claim when we look at a parallel verse:

- "Do you think that I have come to give peace on earth? No, I tell you, but rather division. For from now on in one house there will be five divided, three against two and two against three. They will be divided, father against son and son against father, mother against daughter and daughter against mother, mother-in-law against her daughter-in-law and daughter-in-law against mother-in-law." (Luke 12:51-53)

From these verses, we understand that Jesus used the image of the sword to connote spiritual division, not warfare.

Returning now to the question of giving, should we give indiscriminately? I began to see that if we are to pattern our lives after God, we must exercise wisdom and discernment. Looking back once again at Luke 6, we see that Jesus concluded His teaching with a principle which should guide our giving:

- "Do to others as you would have them do to you. If you love those who love you, what credit is that to you? Even 'sinners' love those who love them. And if you do good to those who are good to you, what credit is that to you? Even 'sinners' do that. And if you lend to those from whom you expect repayment, what credit is that to you? Even 'sinners' lend to 'sinners,' expecting to be repaid in full. But love your enemies, do good to them, and lend to them without expecting to get anything back. Then your reward will be great, and you will be sons of the Most High, because he is kind to the ungrateful and wicked. Be merciful, just as your Father is merciful." (Luke 6:31-36)

Often, Jesus gives us a key to unlock an interpretation. That is what He seems to have done in this case. I began to comprehend what He was saying when I realized that I am compelled to be merciful, just as the "Father is merciful." When I saw His teaching on giving in the light of this over-arching principle, what He said began to make sense. Because of His great mercy, the Father would never give us something that would hurt or destroy either us or others. Such malignant giving could never be in accordance with His will:

- And this is the confidence that we have toward him, that if we ask anything according to his will he hears us. And if we know that he hears us in whatever we ask, we know that we have the requests that we have asked of him. (1 John 5:14-15)

God does not give indiscriminately—and neither should we. If giving is not in the best interests of the other person, then we shouldn't give. I had to learn the difference between destructive, disempowering, indulgent giving and giving that would bless. For example, Paul had argued against the church supporting certain widows. His reasoning? It is a widow's family that should support her when necessary, as we can see in 1 Timothy 5:3-8.

In Luke 6:36, Jesus argued that our mercy should reflect the wisdom of God's mercy. What exactly does that look like? It looks exactly like what is recorded in the Hebrew Scriptures. There, we find *giving accompanied by accountability*. In a most loving way, God displayed a major interest in the welfare of the poor and needy. He did this by requiring that the fields be available to the poor so that they could glean the remains of what was harvested (Leviticus 19:10). He chose not to give handouts to the poor; He knew that this would take away their motivation to work.

It eventually became apparent to me that if I took Jesus' words about giving literally, I would in fact violate other biblical commands. For example, if a friend asked me for my gun so that he could shoot his wife, such "giving" would violate the law against murder. If I gave someone money to buy street drugs, I would be contributing to a possible overdose and criminality. Perhaps an interpretation of Scripture that appears to be ridiculous is in fact ridiculous…and completely wrong-headed.

It must be admitted—we do have a weighty responsibility for the poor. But this responsibility must be exercised wisely, lovingly, and according to the Bible's precepts.

❖ ❖ ❖

Let us revisit our conversation with Bob and his charge that if we are followers of Jesus, we should live as pacifists and never retaliate. According to this line of thinking, we should allow ISIS and its cohorts to continue doing their malevolent best, unopposed.

For years, I struggled with Jesus' elusive teachings. For example, I wondered whether I should turn my cheek—according to Matthew 5:39—when my students were misbehaving. Should I ignore it when a student had even reached the point of threatening others? Fortunately for all concerned, I decided against this kind of "turning the other cheek." It would have brought utter contempt, not only on me, but upon my faith as well.

Seen from the point of view of God's entire revelation, "turning the other cheek" was not meant to be a command calling for the firing of every policeman or the tearing down of every jail. Instead, it was a warning against private citizens taking the law into their own hands to seek revenge. As we can plainly see in Romans 13:1-4, it is the civil magistrate who is to avenge wrongdoing, and not a gang of vigilantes.

Bob would most likely not sit still for an explanation like this. But as I study these verses, I can rest assured that I am not being a hypocrite in what I believe or in the way I act on those beliefs.

❖ ❖ ❖

So then, how are we to understand Jesus if He spoke in parables? We can understand what Jesus said by understanding the Scriptures He embraced—the entire Jewish canon, all the Law and the Prophets—as He clearly declared in Matthew 5:17-19. In short, like Jesus, we must honor and embrace every Word that came from God:

- But he answered [the devil], "It is written, 'Man shall not live by bread alone, but by every word that comes from the mouth of God.'" (Matthew 4:4)

Therefore, we do not possess the privilege of discarding any verse of Scripture. Jesus demonstrated this principle in many ways. He continually quoted or alluded to Scripture, as if to say, "If the Scripture says it, that settles it." He was so saturated with Scripture in its various forms that He often expressed Himself accordingly. Furthermore, Jesus never contradicted the Scriptures. Had He done so, the religious leaders would have quickly brought Him up on charges of blasphemy, something they were never able to do.

We are impelled to view Jesus through the lens of the Scriptures.

Reflecting once again on "turning the other cheek," this idea has often been used to argue that Jesus was teaching pacifism and absolute non-violence. If so, this would mean that He was also proclaiming the end of capital punishment. However, Jesus might have had in mind Job 16:10 and Lamentations 3:30— verses that equate the "striking of the cheek" with insults rather than literal blows. In light of those teachings, to "turn the other cheek" would mean enduring an insult rather than retaliating physically.

Actually, Jesus seems to have endorsed the Hebrew Scripture's teachings in favor of capital punishment. When the Pharisees criticized Jesus' disciples for not following the "traditions of the elders," Jesus retorted:

- "For God commanded, 'Honor your father and your mother,' and, 'Whoever reviles father or mother must surely die.' But you say, 'If anyone tells his father or his mother, "What you would have gained from me is given to God," he need not honor his father.' So for the sake of your tradition you have made void the word of God." (Matthew 15:4-6)

Thus, we can see that Jesus affirmed the fact that reviling one's parents was a capital offense, according to God's Word in Leviticus 20:9. Furthermore, this Scriptural position was to be honored above any tradition. Evidently, Jesus was not teaching absolute non-violence.

Others have made the claim that Jesus never taught in favor of self-defense, but this also is not true. Instead, Jesus seemed to affirm that a husband had a duty to defend his household:

- "Therefore, stay awake, for you do not know on what day your Lord is coming. But know this, that if the master of the house had known in what part of the night the thief was coming, he would have stayed awake and would not have let his house be broken into." (Matthew 24:42-43)

Clearly, Jesus approved of a father defending his family from an intruder. And how could we ever forget the way that Jesus forcefully drove the money-changers from the Temple in John 2? So much for the idea of a passive, non-violent Jesus!

When we understand Jesus' teachings in light of the Hebrew Scriptures, what He said begins to make sense.

❖ ❖ ❖

Here is yet another principle from the OT that would be good for us to keep in mind: There is a strong distinction between the behavior of individuals and the government. Individuals were to love their enemies:

- "If you see the donkey of one who hates you lying down under its burden, you shall refrain from leaving him with it; you shall rescue it with him." (Exodus 23:5)

In light of this, there is no way to conclude—as some do—that Jesus was inventing an entirely new revelation of love...apart from Scripture. Instead, He tried to bring the Israelites back to the true meaning of love found in the OT. Even the "righteous" Pharisees had lost touch with Scripture's teachings on love. Therefore, Jesus corrected them:

- "You have heard that it was said [by the Pharisees], 'You shall love your neighbor and hate your enemy.' But I say to you, Love your enemies and pray for those who persecute you, so that you may be sons of your Father who is in heaven. For he makes his sun rise on the evil and on the good, and sends rain on the just and on the unjust." (Matthew 5:43-45)

The Pharisees were powerless to argue against this logic. They knew that Jesus' words reflected the clear teaching of the Scriptures:

- The LORD is good to all, and his mercy is over all that he has made. (Psalm 145:9)

Likewise, we also need to understand the idea of "turning the other cheek" from the perspective of the Hebrew Scriptures. If we don't look at this in the right way, it appears as if Jesus is replacing what seems to be a barbaric OT teaching—"An eye for an eye"—with another equally unsatisfactory instruction:

- "You have heard that it was said, 'An eye for an eye and a tooth for a tooth.' But I say to you, Do not resist the one who is evil. But if anyone slaps you on the right cheek, turn to him the other also." (Matthew 5:38-39)

Was Jesus replacing an archaic principle of the OT with a new law that commanded absolute non-retaliation? Considering once again my classroom situation, did Jesus' teaching mean that I was to simply love my students and refuse to address any of their wrong-doing?

As time went by and as experience has shown me, I became convinced that such an interpretation would violate Jesus' intent. I had to decide whether or not Jesus' teaching was meant to correct the Mosaic Covenant...or *the current understanding of it*. For one thing, when Jesus cited "An eye for an eye," He did not say, "It is written." Rather, He said, "You have heard that it was said." This spoke volumes to me. Jesus was not taking issue with Mosaic Law but with *the way that it had been misappropriated.* This teaching of Moses was never meant to justify revenge and vigilantism.

Thus, I was able to see that the principle of "An eye for an eye" was not at all barbaric. Instead, the over-arching idea behind these words is this—*the penalty must match the crime*:

- "Eye for eye, tooth for tooth, hand for hand, foot for foot, burn for burn, wound for wound, stripe for stripe. When a man strikes the eye of his slave, male or female, and destroys it, he shall let the slave go free because of his eye. If he knocks out the tooth of his slave, male or female, he shall let the slave go free because of his tooth." (Exodus 21:24-27)

Instead of the slave-master losing his eye, something more in line with justice and compassion was demanded. The master would be compelled to set his slave free, to his own great loss.

Moreover, I eventually came to understand that Jesus *never* criticized the Old Testament:

- "Do not think that I have come to abolish the Law or the Prophets; I have not come to abolish them but to fulfill them. I tell you the truth, until heaven and earth disappear, not the smallest letter, not the least stroke of a pen, will by any means disappear from the Law until everything is accomplished. Anyone who breaks one of the least of these commandments and teaches others to do the same will be called least in the kingdom of heaven, but whoever practices and teaches these commands will be called great in the kingdom of heaven." (Matthew 5:17-19)

Jesus always quoted the Hebrew Scriptures affirmatively. It became obvious to me that the Sermon on the Mount was not an indictment of the Mosaic legal system—as some say—but of our personal abuses of it. In this case, it seems likely that Jesus was taking aim at those who invoked "An eye for an eye" to justify *taking personal revenge*. If this is so, then Jesus was teaching that it is better for us to allow ourselves to be defrauded and insulted, rather than to retaliate.

God Himself would avenge through the governmental authority He had established, a civil order that Jesus affirmed, which included the Sanhedrin:

- "The scribes and the Pharisees sit on Moses' seat, so do and observe whatever they tell you, but not the works they do..." (Matthew 23:2-3a)

As Paul declared, the government is God's instrument to avenge:

- Let every person be subject to the governing authorities. For there is no authority except from God, and those that exist have been instituted by God. Therefore whoever resists the authorities resists what God has appointed, and those who resist will incur judgment. For rulers are not a terror to good conduct, but to bad. Would you have no fear of the one who is in authority? Then do what is good, and you will receive his approval, for he is God's servant for your good. But if you do wrong, be afraid, for he does not bear the sword in vain. For he is the servant of God, an avenger who carries out God's wrath on the wrongdoer. (Romans 13:1-4)

As a Christian and a private citizen, I cannot avenge. Rather, God has ordained the courts to avenge. Perhaps then, I should regard the school system as part of God's "governing authorities" and myself—as a teacher—a minister of His wrath. In this capacity, I am not required to "turn the other cheek." I should take all the steps necessary to assure that my classroom does not descend into chaos.

Likewise, as a private citizen, I am in no position to wage war against ISIS. But the government—under God's authority and operating as "an avenger who carries out God's wrath on the wrongdoer"—should indeed wage a just war against those who do wrong.

❖ ❖ ❖

Jesus also said many other perplexing things—things that do not seem to be in accord with the Scriptures:

- "And when you pray, you must not be like the hypocrites. For they love to stand and pray in the synagogues and at the street corners, that they may be seen by others. Truly, I say to you, they have received their reward. But when you pray, go into your room and shut the door and pray to your Father who is in secret. And your Father who sees in secret will reward you." (Matthew 6:5-6)

This teaching seems to contradict Jesus' request for prayer in the Garden of Gethsemane. And what about all the times that He prayed in public? How are we to understand His command to "shut the door and pray...in secret"? When we examine the context of this teaching, we discover that Jesus' concern is the natural, default tendency we all have to want to be seen and approved by men rather than God:

- "Beware of practicing your righteousness before other people in order to be seen by them, for then you will have no reward from your Father who is in heaven." (Matthew 6:1)

All of us generally tend to be self-righteous. Sometimes we even demand and manipulate the approval of others in order that we might sustain our inflated and insatiable egos. This cancer permeates all areas of our lives—even our prayers—and deserves to be exposed. But how can that happen? Just try praying in private! Do we find that we are less motivated to pray when we are in our "prayer closets"? Could it be that we too want to be seen by men and less-so by God? Perhaps we can understand Jesus' command to pray in our closets as an exercise in self-discovery.

I regard Jesus as the ultimate Doctor of the soul. He wanted His followers to understand the depths of their self-righteous tumors. Therefore, some of His commands that touch on the deep places in our hearts can often be perplexing:

- "But when you give to the needy, do not let your left hand know what your right hand is doing, so that your giving may be in secret. And your Father who sees in secret will reward you." (Matthew 6:3)

Literally, this is absurd. Our hands know nothing, and we cannot hide any giving we do…from ourselves. Jesus' point here is to remind and help us to be keenly aware of *why we are giving*. Is it for the approval of men or of God? In the same way that He admonished us to pray "in secret," here he tells us to give in absolute secrecy. If we rebel against doing this, it probably means that our primary motivation is to look good before others. When we figure this out about ourselves, we will realize how unworthy we are in so many areas before God. This new insight should encourage us once again to put all of our hope in Him. His approval—and His alone—should be our only concern.

❖ ❖ ❖

Ultimately, understanding the teachings of Jesus is all about context. It must determine how we understand any one passage. This same principle of context and its primary importance pertains to the interpretation of all literature, not just the Bible. We are not trying to make a special allowance for the study of our holy book.

Likewise, to apply any one law, a lawyer has to understand how that law has been applied in many different circumstances. Furthermore, the applications and interpretations of any law are not all listed in one place. If we remove any one verse from the context of the rest of the Bible, we will most definitely encounter interpretive problems. For example, one of the Ten Commandments reads, "Thou shall not kill." In the particular Exodus context where that commandment is found, there is no listing of the many exceptions. However, we know that there are a number of caveats to this law that may be found throughout the Bible. There are sanctions for self-defense, warfare, and even capital punishment. And yet, it is impossible to find all of the exceptions for this precept in any one verse or chapter.

Therefore, this same principle—Scripture interprets Scripture— applies throughout the Bible.

Here is one verse that has been cited by some as a clear contradiction:

- "Even so, when you see all these things, you know that it is near, right at the door. I tell you the truth, this generation will certainly not pass away until all these things have happened." (Matthew 24:33-34)

For Bible critic and agnostic Bart D. Ehrman, this verse proves that Jesus was wrong about eschatological timing:

- Jesus fully expected that the history of the world as we know it (as well as how he knew it) was going to come to a screeching halt, that God was soon going to intervene in the affairs of this world, overthrow the forces of evil in a cosmic act of judgment, and destroy huge masses of humanity...Moreover, Jesus expected this cataclysmic end of history would come in his own generation, at least during the lifetime of his disciples. (Ehrman, Bart D. *Jesus: Apocalyptic Prophet of the New Millennium.* Oxford University Press, 1999, p. x)

However, in order to make his case, Ehrman had to ignore several key elements. For one thing, immediately after what He said in vs. 33-34, Jesus said that *He did not know the time of His return:*

- "No one knows about that day or hour, not even the angels in heaven, nor the Son, but only the Father." (Matthew 24:36)

Even more significantly, Ehrman closed his eyes to other elements within the immediate context of Matthew 24, including verses which argue in favor of an extended period of time prior to Jesus' second coming:

- "You will hear of wars and rumors of wars, but see to it that you are not alarmed. Such things must happen, *but the end is still to come*. Nation will rise against nation, and kingdom against kingdom. There will be famines and earthquakes in various places. *All these are the beginning of birth pains*. Then you will be handed over to be persecuted and put to death, and you will be hated by all nations because of me. At that time many will turn away from the faith and will betray and hate each other...*And this gospel of the kingdom will be preached in the whole world as a testimony to all nations, and then the end will come*." (Matthew 24:6-10, 14, emphasis added)

These verses point to *a distant coming*—a coming that would follow the death of the Apostles, a great falling away from the faith, and the Gospel having been preached throughout the "whole world."

What then could Jesus possibly have meant when He stated in Matthew 24:34 that "...this generation will certainly not pass away until all these things have happened"? Here are two possibilities:

1. The Hebrew word for "generation," *dor*, can also be understood as "descendants" or "lineage." It is likely that the Greek word *genea*, for "generation" in Matthew 24:34, can also be understood in this way. In this case, perhaps Jesus was indicating that the descendants of Abraham—the Jews—would not pass away before His return.

2. The "return" of which Jesus was speaking might not have been a reference to His second coming, but rather to the coming judgment of God against Jerusalem in 70 AD. Many of Jesus' disciples would still have been alive at this point in time.

There might even be a third possibility that is better than the ones I have already mentioned. However, here is what is clear: Bart Ehrman's facile conclusion that Jesus was wrong in Matthew 24 ignores much of what is germane to the discussion. In other words, by ignoring the context of Jesus' words, Ehrman is manufacturing a contradiction where none exists.

❖ ❖ ❖

Interpreting and understanding the teachings of Jesus can be a lengthy and arduous undertaking. But let us take heart—the Lord helps us in this marvelous endeavor:

- It was he who gave some to be apostles, some to be prophets, some to be evangelists, and some to be pastors and teachers, to prepare God's people for works of service, so that the body of Christ may be built up until we all reach unity in the faith and in the knowledge of the Son of God and become mature, attaining to the whole measure of the fullness of Christ. Then we will no longer be infants, tossed back and forth by the waves, and blown here and there by every wind of teaching and by the cunning and craftiness of men in their deceitful scheming. (Ephesians 4:11-14)

Chapter 16

UNDERSTANDING JESUS' PROMISES

CHAPTER SUMMARY

Although Jesus' promise to give us whatever we ask might seem unconditional, there are indeed some conditions attached. The phrase "in My name" is loaded with premises and provisos. Our prayers must be in accordance with His will.

People interpret Jesus differently. Some believe that He has promised to give us whatever we want. For proof, they cite this passage:

- "Ask, and it will be given to you; seek, and you will find; knock, and it will be opened to you. For everyone who asks receives, and the one who seeks finds, and to the one who knocks it will be opened." (Matthew 7:7-8)

From these verses, it appears as if there are no stipulations or limitations associated with Jesus' promise. Could it possibly be that there are no conditions to be met before our prayers are answered? If we read just a few more verses in the same passage, it turns out that there is in fact a proviso—God gives "good things":

- "If you then, who are evil, know how to give good gifts to your children, how much more will your Father who is in heaven give good things to those who ask him!" (Matthew 7:11)

157

This means that if you pray for a gun to kill your wife, or for a bag of street drugs, you will not be getting your prayers answered. The reason? Simply this: God does not consider these items to be "good things."

James attaches a similar limitation to God's giving:

- You ask and do not receive, because you ask wrongly, to spend it on your passions. (James 4:3)

According to James, our motives must be right when we make our requests in prayer. However, the so-called "prosperity gospel" ministers regard prayer in an entirely different way. To back up the validity of their point of view, they cite other promises of Jesus:

- "Whatever you ask in my name, this I will do, that the Father may be glorified in the Son. If you ask me anything in my name, I will do it." (John 14:13-14)

Here again, there is a condition to be met which some people conveniently overlook. Jesus will grant our requests in order that..."the Father may be glorified." Praying for a bag of street drugs does not glorify the Father.

There is a common phrase that always manages to surface in these discussions—"anything in my name." There is no doubt that this is indeed an important phrase. On a number of occasions, Jesus Himself referred to the "name":

- "You did not choose me, but I chose you and appointed you that you should go and bear fruit and that your fruit should abide, so that whatever you ask the Father in my name, he may give it to you." (John 15:16)

One chapter later, Jesus said:

- "In that day you will ask nothing of me. Truly, truly, I say to you, whatever you ask of the Father in my name, he will give it to you. Until now you have asked nothing in my name. Ask, and you will receive, that your joy may be full." (John 16:23-24)

After reading these verses, the obvious question that comes to mind is, "What does it mean to 'ask…in my name'?" While it might seem as if this promise gives us a blank check, it does not. The phrase "in my name" implies conditions. Getting our prayers answered is not a matter of simply saying the word, "Jesus." In fact, few of us take this literally. If we did, we would have to pronounce Jesus' Hebrew name, being extra careful to pronounce it in the absolutely correct manner. And who knows the way that Jesus Himself pronounced it!

Instead, in Hebraic thinking, one's name represented what the person was. Jacob, meaning "usurper," was so named because it seemed like he was trying to take the place of his twin brother Esau, who had emerged from the womb first. Jacob's hand had been on his brother's ankle, and he appeared to be pulling Esau back so that he could be born first and thus claim the rights of the "firstborn." In fact, if we study the life of Jacob, we learn that he had a pattern of trying to take what didn't belong to him. Jacob's name reflected Jacob's nature.

Likewise, the name of Jesus represents His divine nature and will. When He announced the Great Commission, Jesus sent out His Apostles with these instructions:

- "Go therefore and make disciples of all nations, baptizing them *in the name* of the Father and of the Son and of the Holy Spirit…" (Matthew 28:19, emphasis added)

In this verse, "name" is in the singular, signifying that the Father, Son, and Spirit all share the same name. They clearly do not share the name "Jesus." What, then, is the "name" that they share? Going back to our word study, we would say that they all share the same character and, of course, divinity.

After declaring several of His "in my name" promises, Jesus prayed to the Father, referring specifically to His "name":

- "I have manifested your name to the people whom you gave me out of the world. Yours they were, and you gave them to me, and they have kept your word." (John 17:6)

Which "name" did Jesus manifest to His disciples? It could not have been "Yahweh," since this name does not appear in the Greek New Testament. Neither could it have been "Elohim" or "Adonai," for the same reason. Instead, Jesus manifested the Father Himself, as the NIV suggests in its translation of the same verse:

- "I have revealed *you* to those you gave me out of the world..." (John 17:6a, emphasis added)

When one carefully examines the context of Jesus' words in these verses, there is another insight to glean. It seems as if the manifestation of God's name was closely related to the Apostles and their commitment to keeping His Word, as we see in John 17:6b. This suggests that by revealing the name of the Father, Jesus was also revealing His Word—a Word that is necessary for salvation and a Word that must be kept.

Later on in the same chapter, Jesus prayed that His revelation of the Father—His name—would continue so that His love might be in those who followed Him:

- "I made known to them your name, and I will continue to make it known, that the love with which you have loved me may be in them, and I in them." (John 17:26)

The revelation of Jesus' name, which includes His will and character as well as the Gospel message, is clearly necessary for salvation. John makes this very clear in the following verse:

- ...but these are written so that you may believe that Jesus is the Christ, the Son of God, and that by believing you may have life in his name. (John 20:31; see also Luke 24:47; Acts 4:12)

The name to which John refers, in which there is life, could not simply have been a matter of uttering J-E-S-U-S. Many in His day were known by the name "Jesus." Calling out to any one of them could never bring salvation. Instead, His name represented everything about Jesus—His character, His Word, and His Gospel. Therefore, when we ask for anything in His name, we are asking according to Jesus and all that He represents. No blank check here!

There are many other examples of the way that the New Testament Scriptures portray God's name as representing God Himself. Let us take a fresh look at a very familiar verse:

- ...for, "Everyone who calls on the name of the Lord will be saved." (Romans 10:13, citing Joel 2:32)

Our salvation is a matter of calling upon the Lord Himself, not just repeating a name—Jesus—which was shared by many others. Jesus clearly taught that the mere recitation of a name would never save anyone:

- "Not everyone who says to me, 'Lord, Lord,' will enter the kingdom of heaven, but the one who does the will of my Father who is in heaven. On that day many will say to me, 'Lord, Lord, did we not prophesy in your name, and cast out demons in your name, and do many mighty works in your name?' And then will I declare to them, 'I never knew you; depart from me, you workers of lawlessness.'" (Matthew 7:21-23)

It is only a true faith in the divine Person of Jesus—as evidenced by obedience—that is able to save us. Calling upon the name of the Lord is a pledge of our obedience to do the will of the Father. And once again, when we call upon the name of Jesus in a biblical sense, we are calling upon the Person of Jesus and all that He represents.

The same principle applies to prayer "in my name." While it is a good idea to pray "in Jesus' name," this phrase requires that we ask according to the character, plan, and will of the Father and the Son. Outside of what His name actually represents, there are no blank checks available. Simply uttering the name of Jesus will not open any doors.

The sons of Sceva paid a high price when they tried to cast out a demon with nothing more than the verbalization of a name:

- Then some of the itinerant Jewish exorcists undertook to invoke the name of the Lord Jesus over those who had evil spirits, saying, "I adjure you by the Jesus whom Paul proclaims." Seven sons of a Jewish high priest named Sceva were doing this. But the evil spirit answered them, "Jesus I know, and Paul I recognize, but who are you?" And the man in whom was the evil spirit leaped on them, mastered all of them and overpowered them, so that they fled out of that house naked and wounded. (Acts 19:13-16)

In His final conversation with His disciples, before the Garden of Gethsemane, Jesus declared:

- "If you abide in me, and my words abide in you, ask whatever you wish, and it will be done for you. By this my Father is glorified, that you bear much fruit and so prove to be my disciples." (John 15:7-8)

Receiving anything from God depends upon abiding in His words. This entails obedience. Consequently, when we obey, we will "bear much fruit." Whatever a person sows, he will also reap. If we honor God, He will also honor us. Therefore, wasting our prayers on our lusts is not a biblical option. In our prayers, we are to ask that we might be fruitful for the sake of the glory of the Father.

In the Sermon on the Mount, Jesus taught us:

- "But seek first the kingdom of God and his righteousness, and all these things will be added to you." (Matthew 6:33)

Receiving "all these things" depends upon honoring God above everything else in our lives. It means putting His will above our own, as Jesus had. It is true that God's ultimate purpose is to one day give us the world. But before that day dawns, He is preparing us. How? By teaching us to be servants:

- Jesus said to him, "No one who puts his hand to the plow and looks back is fit for the kingdom of God." (Luke 9:62)

These are strong words. Clearly, before all else, we have to be about the Lord's business. This leaves little room for the teachings of those who preach that we have been given a blank check and all we need to do is claim it.

Chapter 17

UNDERSTANDING JESUS' MANNER OF ARGUMENTATION

CHAPTER SUMMARY

Often, Jesus talked to His opponents from the perspective of their errant worldview. In effect, He was saying, "Let me show you how your beliefs fail you." If we do not recognize Jesus' polemic strategy, we will fail to understand what He is communicating.

Unless I am talking to someone who might be receptive to the Gospel, I usually begin by showing them the problems with their own hopes and beliefs. Why do I do this? People will not receive the Good News unless they are convinced that they need it.

Today, the vast majority of people believe in moral relativism. From this perspective, morality is just something we make up to serve our needs. For those in this "camp," morality does not have an independent existence. It is dependent on factors like what we decide to live by and how we were raised.

According to this mind-set, there is no objective or absolute moral standard by which we can judge others. Therefore, we cannot judge a Hitler or an Osama Bin Laden, since there is nothing that makes our moral judgments any more valid than theirs. If I have this frame of reference, I might try to teach my children that they shouldn't steal or bully. However, I cannot teach them these principles on the basis of what is right and wrong or what is just or unjust. After all, these concepts are merely *ideas that we have created.* So, I am forced to appeal to the self-interest of my children:

> *Johnny, don't steal—your self-esteem will suffer. Don't be a bully or someone will bully you.*

In my conversations with those who are moral relativists, I try to show the inadequacies or fallacies of their beliefs. I do this, hoping that they might become receptive to better beliefs—specifically, a belief system and morality from above!

This was often the strategy of Jesus. He would ask His opponents to state the source of their hopes and beliefs and then demonstrate how these paradigms invariably fail.

A lawyer tested Jesus with the question: "What must I do to inherit eternal life?" Instead of telling the man to believe in Him, Jesus asked him to state his thoughts on the subject, something the lawyer was happy to do:

- He [Jesus] said to him, "What is written in the Law? How do you read it?" And he answered, "You shall love the Lord your God with all your heart and with all your soul and with all your strength and with all your mind, and your neighbor as yourself." And he said to him, "You have answered correctly; do this, and you will live." (Luke 10:26-28)

Admittedly, we tend to stumble over these words. It seems as if Jesus was actually endorsing the man's worldview, affirming salvation by keeping the Law. But Jesus was only trying to lead him into deeper truths about the ways of God. Jesus knew that the man had little understanding of grace—he was convinced that he could earn his way to heaven through keeping the Law. He believed he was entitled to heaven and had little need for the mercy of God, the hope that Jesus had come to offer. That is why he was content to merely test Jesus. He even went so far as to try to justify himself by asking who his neighbor was.

Since Jesus perceived that the lawyer was not amenable to the Good News, He had to first demonstrate that the man's hope was baseless. He did this through a parable. If the lawyer expected to earn eternal life, he would have to live as sacrificially as the Good Samaritan. After Jesus had shared the parable, He concluded with the admonition to "Go and do likewise" (Luke 10: 37b). We should understand these words to mean: "Go and do likewise, since you believe that this is the way that eternal life can be earned."

Of course, we should all do as the Good Samaritan had done, but we would never be able to earn eternal life in this manner. Instead, by attempting to live this way, it would soon become glaringly evident that we are spiritual failures who cannot earn any blessing whatsoever from God. We are blessed by grace and not by merit.

If we fail to understand how Jesus argued or tried to share the Good News, we will be confused about a number of His teachings. They will appear to us as directly opposed to much of what He said about salvation by grace through faith (John 3:16; 5:24; 6:29; 8:24).

❖ ❖ ❖

Sometimes Jesus utilized highly unexpected means to contend for God. Once, He had literally called a Canaanite Gentile woman a "dog" and therefore ineligible to receive any of the blessings of God:

- He answered, "I was sent only to the lost sheep of the house of Israel." But she came and knelt before him, saying, "Lord, help me." And he answered, "It is not right

to take the children's bread and throw it to the dogs."
(Matthew 15:24-26)

This seems to contradict a host of Jesus' other teachings and
actions. Clearly, Jesus regarded the Gentiles to be just as
eligible for salvation as the Jews. Just two verses later, He even
declared that this Gentile woman's faith was great, something
He had never said to His own Apostles or to any other Jew
(Matthew 15:28; see also 8:10). Furthermore, when Jesus
announced His Great Commission, He sent His disciples out
into the world of the Gentiles (Matthew 28:19-20). This seeming
contradiction led one theologian to call Jesus a recovering
racist. However, there is another way to understand this
account which is more in keeping with the teachings of
Scripture.

As we consider this passage, we must keep in mind that Jesus'
own disciples were His opponents. They were the racists who
looked down on Gentiles as "dogs" and not deserving of
anything from God. That is why He, wanting to show His
disciples the fallacy of their beliefs, purposely took them on a
trip to Tyre and Sidon in Phoenicia—Gentile territory.

When the woman began to cry out to Jesus, the disciples
wanted Him to send the woman away. They regarded her as a
nuisance. At first, Jesus played along with them and did not
answer her. Then, He referred to her as a dog, undeserving of
any bread. However, in her response, she proved that she had
more wisdom, understanding, and faith than Jesus' own
disciples. This incident proved that the worldview of the
disciples was totally mistaken.

❖ ❖ ❖

When the religious leadership criticized Jesus for hanging out
with sinners, Jesus replied to them according to their own
beliefs:

- And Jesus answered them, "Those who are well have no need of a physician, but those who are sick. I have not come to call the righteous but sinners to repentance." (Luke 5:31-32)

From this, we might be tempted to think that Jesus regarded the scribes and Pharisees as "righteous." However, in view of the rest of His teachings, it is clear that He did not. He was merely showing them the fallacy of their thinking. Since the Pharisees regarded these sinners as truly sick, wouldn't it be appropriate for Jesus, the Great Physician, to tend to them? Of course! In this way, Jesus showed the Pharisees that they had absolutely no reason to criticize Him in this regard.

The religious leadership of the day would often bring this charge against Jesus:

- And the Pharisees and the scribes grumbled, saying, "This man receives sinners and eats with them." (Luke 15:2)

Once again, to illustrate that their beliefs were baseless and even anti-Scriptural, Jesus told the parables of the lost coin and the lost sheep, concluding:

- "Just so, I tell you, there will be more joy in heaven over one sinner who repents than over ninety-nine righteous persons who need no repentance." (Luke 15:7; see also vs. 8-10)

Did Jesus actually believe that there were some righteous people who did not need repentance? No! Clearly, Jesus believed that all needed to repent (Luke 13:1-5; 24:47). The Pharisees, however, believed that they were above that sort of thing. Jesus wanted to show them that their opinion of sinners did not comport with the assessment of the heavenly beings, who find great joy "over one sinner who repents" (Luke 15:7).

It is important that we do not take Jesus' teachings out of context. If we do, as in this case, we might tragically conclude that some people do not need to repent. This is just one more example proving that we must interpret every verse of Scripture by the light shed from other verses.

❖ ❖ ❖

For one final illustration, let us examine the narrative of a rich young man who came to Jesus to ask Him about the way to eternal life:

- And as he was setting out on his journey, a man ran up and knelt before him and asked him, "Good Teacher, what must I do to inherit eternal life?" And Jesus said to him, "Why do you call me good? No one is good except God alone. You know the commandments: 'Do not murder, Do not commit adultery, Do not steal, Do not bear false witness, Do not defraud, Honor your father and mother.'" (Mark 10:17-19)

Although this man had sincerely inquired about eternal life, it became clear that he—like the lawyer in Luke 10—actually believed that heaven was a reward that could be earned. In fact, he believed that he was entitled to it because he had kept all the commandments from the time when he was yet a boy. However, he was in denial about his true status before God. For example, had the young man been able to fully obey Jesus' teaching in Matthew 5 about murder in the heart or adultery in the mind? Of course not!

Perceiving this, Jesus understood that he wasn't yet ready to hear the Gospel. He had to first be shown that his hope in law-keeping was illusory, and that he too needed the mercy of God. Therefore, Jesus had to bring this man back to the letter of the Law…to show him that he was unable to keep it:

- And Jesus, looking at him, loved him, and said to him, "You lack one thing: go, sell all that you have and give to the poor, and you will have treasure in heaven; and come, follow me." (Mark 10:21)

Could obedience to this directive bring the young man to eternal life? No, not by itself. However, Jesus' challenge brought this man to despair and thus one step closer to the Gospel and his need for the mercy of God. In other words, Jesus used the man's unfounded hope to bring him to despair and—hopefully—closer to being open to the one true Hope.

If we fail to fully comprehend Jesus' strategy, we will conclude wrongly that He was teaching a salvation by law-keeping. This would be in direct opposition to, not only Jesus' other teachings, but the teachings of the rest of the New Testament as well (Romans 3:10-23; Galatians 2:16).

❖ ❖ ❖

I must admit that interpretation can sometimes be truly demanding. Once again, it is for this reason that God has given us pastors and teachers—to lead us to a true knowledge of God through His Word (Ephesians 4:11-14).

Chapter 18

UNDERSTANDING THE SEVEN CHURCHES OF THE BOOK OF REVELATION

CHAPTER SUMMARY

The teachings on the Seven Churches of Revelation offer deep and valuable lessons about faith, salvation, overcoming, tolerance, and repentance. They also help us to understand how the Lord regards our own churches.

Interpreting the Book of Revelation is challenging. A good place to begin is with the letters to the seven churches found in Chapters 2 and 3. Several commonalities strike us immediately. Each of the letters is addressed "To the angel [singular] of the church in…" one of seven different locations in Asia Minor, present-day western Turkey. However, it is clear that these letters were intended for a wide readership. This is easy to see by the way that each one of them concludes:

- "He who has an ear, let him hear what the Spirit says to the churches…" (Revelation 2:7a, 11a, 17a, 29; 3:6, 13, 22)

This suggests several things:

1. We need to consider what the Spirit said, not just to one, but all seven churches. That way we can get the big picture. We can see the entire range of the criticism as well as the commendations that were declared by the angel. And, considering the grammatical structure in

each of the Scriptures mentioned above, this is an imperative or command, not simply a suggestion.

2. Not everyone "has an ear" that actually hears. If the message is coming from the Spirit, we can assume that it must be spiritually discerned by those who hear it. We need to thank God that He has cleansed our ears that we may hear what He says—and pray that He will continue to do so.

I know how easy it is to go astray. According to Jeremiah 17:9, the heart is terribly deceitful. I therefore always try to pray that He will lead me into His truth, not only in terms of what I write but also in terms of what I say. I have a terrible habit of responding to challengers on Facebook or on my blog before I pray. By neglecting this very important component of my work, I am essentially telling God, "I can handle this myself." This is a patent contradiction of Scripture which informs us that we can do nothing without Him (John 15:4-5; 2 Corinthians 3:5). I am therefore asking God that He would teach me a greater dependence upon Him.

❖ ❖ ❖

Although each letter ends with the admonition to "hear what the *Spirit* says to the churches," each also states that the message is coming from the risen *Christ*. For instance, the letter to Thyatira in 2:18 reads, "These are the words of *the Son of God*." This is not a contradiction but an assertion that the Spirit and Christ are One.

These seven letters also conclude with a promise of great blessing to those who "overcome." As we study these blessings, we realize that they are all related. They are all part of a package deal called "salvation," or, "eternal life in Christ Jesus":

1. In the letter to the church in Ephesus, the overcomers are promised "…the right to eat from the tree of life, which is in the paradise of God" (Revelation 2:7). This is the promise of eternal life.

2. To the church in Smyrna, the overcomers are promised that they will not be "…hurt at all by the second death" (Revelation 2:11).

3. The overcomers of the church in Pergamum are promised "hidden manna" (Revelation 2:17), the bread of life.

4. The overcomers of the church in Thyatira are promised "authority over the nations" (Revelation 2:26). This is a promise later affirmed for all believers in Revelation 22:5.

5. The overcomers of the church in Sardis are promised that God "will never blot out his [their] name from the book of life" (Revelation 3:5).

6. The overcomers of the church in Philadelphia are promised that each one of them will be made "a pillar in the temple of my God. Never again will he leave it…" (Revelation 3:12). We will all be priests of God, ministering from the Tree of Life.

7. The overcomers of the church in Laodicea are promised "…to sit with me on my throne" (Revelation 3:21). Once again, this relates to the promise in 22:5 that all believers will reign with Christ.

These promised blessings to those who are overcomers give all of Christ's bondservants the same hope! No matter how good or bad a church has been, the faith and repentance of its members opens the door to eternal life.

❖ ❖ ❖

Now for the big question: What does it mean to be an "overcomer," and how can I be sure that I am one?

There are two passages from 1 John that are particularly illuminating. They help to provide us with a portrait that shows what overcoming looks like:

- You, dear children, are from God and have overcome them, because the one who is in you is greater than the one who is in the world. They are from the world and therefore speak from the viewpoint of the world, and the world listens to them. We are from God, and whoever knows God listens to us; but whoever is not from God does not listen to us. This is how we recognize the Spirit of truth and the spirit of falsehood. (1 John 4:4-6)

- For everyone born of God overcomes the world. This is the victory that has overcome the world, even our faith. Who is it that overcomes the world? Only he who believes that Jesus is the Son of God. (1 John 5:4-5)

Here is what we can take away from these verses about overcomers:

1. Overcomers are all born of God through faith in Christ. Those who are not of God cannot be overcomers.

2. Overcoming is of God. Only He is greater than anything we could possibly encounter that might jeopardize our victory.

3. Overcomers are those who listen to the Apostles and obey God's Word. Those who are not overcomers place other things before God's Word.

4. Overcoming is the same thing as believing and trusting in Christ. Consequently, those who overcome are those who continue to the end (Hebrews 3:6, 14).

This is good news! It does not mean that we must attain a certain level of moral perfection. But it does mean that our life in Christ depends on trusting in Him as He truly is. This, of course, entails repentance. If we refuse to repent of our sins, it means that we are not trusting in Him—we are trusting in something else. If we are trusting in Him, we will do what He tells us to do.

Let me try to illustrate this simple truth with an analogy. If I say that I trust my doctor, but I throw away the pills he prescribed for me, then I don't really trust Him. Likewise, if I trust in Christ but refuse to do what He tells me to do, then I don't really trust in Him. According to John 14:21-24, those who trust Him will keep His Word.

Don't worry if your faith seems flimsy and insubstantial. Don't worry if you struggle with many temptations that vie against your faith. After all, face it—we are powerless to keep our own faith. This is something that God does for us (1 Peter 1:5; Acts 13:48; 16:14; 18:27; Philippians 1:29). If you are not sure that you really want God more than anything else, confess that to Him and ask for His help. He hears our repentant prayers.

❖ ❖ ❖

The Spirit informed five of the seven churches in the Book of Revelation that they needed to repent. Interestingly, the Spirit did not insist on this requirement for the churches in Philadelphia and Smyrna. Clearly, the reason for their exemption could not have been that everyone in those two churches was sinless. We know that anyone who says that he is without sin is either deceiving himself or is a liar (1 John 1:8-10; James 3:2). Instead, we must conclude that the men and women in those churches had repented of their sins and thus had found complete forgiveness and cleansing (1 John 1:9).

Repentance is foundational to the entire Christian life. When someone repents, this constitutes the supreme act of overcoming. In fact, the victory is so glorious that the angels of heaven rejoice:

- "In the same way, I tell you, there is rejoicing in the presence of the angels of God over one sinner who repents." (Luke 15: 10).

The other five churches were instructed to repent because, unlike Smyrna and Philadelphia, they had not yet repented and experienced a total restoration with God.

I had an experience that demonstrates such total restoration. While my wife was driving through heavy traffic on Interstate 80, I was talking to a pastor-friend of mine on the cell phone. The traffic slowed down and came to a dead stop. I became so upset that I forgot that I was talking on the phone and began to curse. Suddenly, to my great embarrassment, I remembered that I was in the middle of a phone call. I apologized profusely but continued to feel humiliated.

Months later, I saw my pastor-friend again and told him what another friend of mine had said about the incident: "Well, I guess that's the last time you'll ever get to speak from his pulpit!" My pastor-friend laughed and assured me that this would not be the case—and it wasn't.

My friend had embodied Christ for me. He showed me the way Christ is with us. When we honestly confess our sins, they are immediately obliterated. We are no longer burdened by their deception, condemnation or contamination. This is how the churches in Philadelphia and Smyrna had overcome, and this is how they could be assured of the glory that awaited them.

❖ ❖ ❖

Three of the churches mentioned in Revelation that had not yet repented were either castigated for their tolerance or commended for their lack thereof. The church in Ephesus had "forsaken [its] first love," but to its credit, the Spirit said:

- "I know your deeds, your hard work and your perseverance. I know that you cannot tolerate wicked men, that you have tested those who claim to be apostles but are not, and have found them false." (Revelation 2:2)

Tolerance has become the chief virtue in our society and even in some of our churches. And yet, there are indeed some things that the Church should not tolerate. For example, according to Revelation 2:6, the Ephesian church hated the "practices of the Nicolaitans." That sounds fairly intolerant, but remember—they were commended for this. On the other hand, churches like the church at Thyatira that tolerated false teaching in their midst were scorned:

- "I know your deeds, your love and faith, your service and perseverance, and that you are now doing more than you did at first. Nevertheless, I have this against you: *You tolerate that woman Jezebel*, who calls herself a prophetess. By her teaching she misleads my servants into sexual immorality and the eating of food sacrificed to idols." (Revelation 2:19-20, emphasis added)

We can see that God was angry with this church. She would need to repent—turning away from her tolerance of sin—to be in right relationship with Him once again.

There is a similar story connected with the church in Pergamum. Although it had been grandly commended, there were those in her midst that were tolerating false, destructive teaching:

- "Nevertheless, I have a few things against you: You have people there who hold to the teaching of Balaam, who taught Balak to entice the Israelites to sin by eating food sacrificed to idols and by committing sexual immorality. Likewise you also have those who hold to the teaching of the Nicolaitans." (Revelation 2:14-15)

And what would be the remedy for this kind of misguided tolerance?

- "Repent therefore! Otherwise I will soon come to you and will fight against them with the sword of my mouth." (Revelation 2:16)

We are our brothers' keepers. We must be concerned about what the brethren teach and believe. We cannot let bygones be bygones. Many have endorsed the false teaching, "Judge not that you not be judged." Jesus was not teaching against all forms of judgment and discernment. He was teaching that we first had to remove our own blindness—the log in our eye—before we could see clearly enough to correct our brother—to remove the splinter from his eye (Matthew 7:1-5). For the sake of appearing to be tolerant and broad-minded, we in the Church tolerate entirely too much falsehood and sin in our midst.

Truth is the growth-food of the church. When this food is withheld or abused, we do not grow. This is why teaching and biblical discipleship have always been central to Christ's Church. Consequently, the early Church "devoted themselves to the apostle's teaching" (Acts 2:42). Likewise, Jesus' Great Commission required His Apostles to go forth, "teaching them [new disciples] to obey everything I have commanded you" (Matthew 28:20). As Paul tearfully departed from the Ephesian elders for the last time, he committed them "…to God and to the word of his grace, which can build you up and give you an inheritance among all those who are sanctified" (Acts 20:32).

If the Word is food, then the perversion of the Word is poison. Therefore, Paul required that the elder...

- ...must hold firmly to the trustworthy message as it has been taught, so that he can encourage others by sound doctrine and refute those who oppose it. For there are many rebellious people, mere talkers and deceivers, especially those of the circumcision group. They must be silenced, because they are ruining whole households by teaching things they ought not to teach... (Titus 1:9-11a)

Love should never tolerate deception and falsehood—they are too destructive. Instead, love must judge and correct. Paul reiterated Jesus' teaching in Matthew 18:15-19 in this way:

- Brothers, if someone is caught in a sin, you who are spiritual should restore him gently. But watch yourself, or you also may be tempted. (Galatians 6:1)

Correcting and restoring a brother to the truth is not optional. Yet, it is also not required of everyone. Only those who are "spiritual"—those who have removed the log from their eye—can see clearly enough to remove the splinter from their brother's eye.

Well then, what does being "spiritual" entail? Repentance, of course! When we are repentant, we acknowledge how needy and fallible we are. We face the ugly truth about ourselves. Humbled by this, we become gentle, since we realize that we too have likewise fallen. Therefore, Paul counsels us to "watch yourself, or you also may be tempted." The one who feels he cannot be tempted is in denial and shouldn't try to correct anyone. If he does, his arrogance will be a turn-off to believers and seekers alike.

❖ ❖ ❖

Even though the churches at Pergamum and Thyatira most definitely had their problems, they were far from the worst churches. Sardis and Laodicea head this list. Their sin was the most grievous and the most dangerous to real spiritual vitality. In fact, the Spirit had reserved His strongest denunciations for these two churches. To Sardis, He wrote:

- "I know your deeds; you have a reputation of being alive, but you are dead." (Revelation 3:1c)

Sardis and Laodicea were the two churches that had received no commendations. Ironically, these were the two churches that had thought well of themselves! Here is what the Spirit said to Laodicea:

- "You say, 'I am rich; I have acquired wealth and do not need a thing.' But you do not realize that you are wretched, pitiful, poor, blind and naked." (Revelation 3:17)

I shudder when I read these denunciations. This is because I know that I too am capable of thinking that I "have a reputation" (Revelation 3:1) and that "I am rich...and do not need a thing." It makes me think of this prayer from the Book of Proverbs:

- Keep falsehood and lies far from me; give me neither poverty nor riches, but give me only my daily bread. Otherwise, I may have too much and disown you and say, 'Who is the LORD?' Or I may become poor and steal, and so dishonor the name of my God. (Proverbs 30:8-9)

Pride is a murderer. It has slain many. It overtook Saul and Solomon. It nearly brought down David. I want this to be the substance of my prayers—that the Lord would only give me my "daily bread" and protect me from a diet that is too heady for me, inclining me to arrogance.

❖ ❖ ❖

Let us now return to the two churches that were not required to repent—Philadelphia and Smyrna. God had protected these churches through a healthy diet of trials. To Smyrna, the Spirit wrote:

- "I know your afflictions and your poverty—yet you are rich!" (Revelation 2:9a)

However, they would not be rich in this life:

- "Do not be afraid of what you are about to suffer. I tell you, the devil will put some of you in prison to test you, and you will suffer persecution for ten days. Be faithful, even to the point of death, and I will give you the crown of life." (Revelation 2:10)

What leanness—our Lord called some from Smyrna to martyrdom!

To Philadelphia, the Spirit wrote: "I know that you have little strength" (Revelation 3:8b). He called upon them to "endure [the hardships] patiently" (Revelation 3:10b). Ironically, those who thought themselves rich and self-sufficient were really poor, while those who regarded themselves as poor and needy were actually rich in the Lord.

Meanwhile, the world calls us to be like Sardis—to believe in ourselves and anything that will boost our self-esteem. Tragically, messages like this are being taught in many of today's churches. The former pastor of the Crystal Cathedral, Robert Schuller, is reported to have preached that...

- "Reformation Theology failed to make clear that the core of sin is a lack of self-esteem…The most serious sin is the one that causes me to say, 'I am unworthy. I may have no claim to divine sonship if you examine me at my worst.' For once a person believes he is an 'unworthy sinner,' it is doubtful if he can really honestly accept the saving grace God offers in Jesus Christ." (Horton, Michael Scott. *The Agony of Deceit.* Moody Press, 1992, p. 136)

However, Jesus consistently taught the very opposite thing:

- "So you also, when you have done all that you were commanded, say, 'We are unworthy servants; we have only done what was our duty.'" (Luke 17:10)

What are we to conclude from this? First of all, we must recognize that it is the Lord Who is our strength, our righteousness, and our protection. When we regard *ourselves* as righteous or worthy, we no longer esteem God in this way and we will be humbled. For we know that God humbles those who exalt themselves so that they might repent (Luke 14:11; 18:14; 1 Peter 5:4-6). But those who humble themselves and clearly see their poverty, He will exalt.

My prayer then is this: "Lord, give me only those things that are good for me. Let me not trust in my own faulty judgment or righteousness but in Yours alone. Let me never think that I am good or worthy of anything from You, but let my hope and my joy be in You alone. In this and in all ways, lead me and guide me in such a way that I might be an overcomer. Amen."

Finally, may the Lord bless His overcomers as we study Scripture on our life-long…

Quest for Understanding!